CHILDREN'S
RESOURCE BOOKS FOR TEACHERS
series editor
ALAN MALEY

PROJECTS WITH YOUNG LEARNERS

Diane Phillips, Sarah Burwood & Helen Dunford

OXFORD
UNIVERSITY PRESS

Oxford University Press
Great Clarendon Street, Oxford OX2 6DP

Oxford New York
Athens Auckland Bangkok Bogotá
Buenos Aires Calcutta Cape Town Chennai
Dar es Salaam Delhi Florence Hong Kong
Istanbul Karachi Kuala Lumpur Madrid
Melbourne Mexico City Mumbai Nairobi
Paris São Paulo Singapore Taipei Tokyo
Toronto Warsaw

and associated companies in
Berlin Ibadan

Oxford and *Oxford English*
are trade marks of Oxford University Press

ISBN 0 19 437221 9

© Oxford University Press 1999

Photocopying

The publisher grants permission for the
photocopying of those items or pages marked
'photocopiable material' according to the
following conditions. Individual purchasers may
make copies for their own use or for use by classes
they teach. School purchasers may make copies
for use by their staff and students, but this
permission does not extend to additional schools
or branches. Under no circumstance may any
part of this book be photocopied for resale.

Illustrations by Margaret Wellbank
Additional illustrations by Mary Burwood
Cover illustration by Val Saunders

Typeset by Wyvern 21 Ltd., Bristol

Printed in Hong Kong

Acknowledgements

We would like to thank all our many colleagues who we have worked with on Bell Young Learners courses. Ideas develop and change from teacher to teacher and from course to course and get better and better. Many of the ideas in this book have been adapted and developed by ourselves and teachers working on our courses. Our special thanks to all those teachers, particularly to Karen Barnes, Rebecca Hudson and Beverly Close, who have all worked on Island projects of different kind in the past, and to Helen Wood who first showed the 'Elect a President' activity when we were working at Studio School together.

The authors and publisher are grateful to those who have given permission to reproduce the following extract of copyright material.

'Happy birthday to you' words and music by Patty S. Hill and Mildred Hill © 1935 (renewed 1962), Summy Birchard Inc., USA and Keith Prowse Music Pub. Co. Ltd., EMI Music Publishing Limited, London WC2H 0EA. Reproduced by permission of IMP Ltd.

Contents

The author and series editor   1

Foreword   3

Introduction   5

How to use this book   8

Project 1 Let's have a party!

Beginner and above 5–9

Description of the project   25

Language and skills grid   26

Activity	*Time (minutes)*	
1.1 Happy birthday	30	28
1.2 Party game—pirates	30	30
1.3 Party masks	45	32
1.4 Party game—animal circle	45	33
1.5 Party song—Old Macdonald had a zoo	30	35
1.6 Party game—pin the tail on the donkey	45	36
1.7 Party crackers	60	38
1.8 Party game—blind man's buff	30	40
1.9 Party food	60	41
1.10 Party invitations	45	42
1.11 More party food	60	44
1.12 Party time!	60	45

Project 2 Block of flats

Elementary and above 8–11

Description of the project   47

Language and skills grid   48

Activity	*Time (minutes)*	
2.1 Rooms in the flat	60	50
2.2 Furniture for the flat	60	52

2.3	Family tree	60	54
2.4	The people who live in the flat	60	57
2.5	Guess who!	60	59
2.6	Pets	60	61
2.7	Lost!	60	62
2.8	Fun club	60	64
2.9	Family scrapbook	As appropriate	66
2.10	Project display	As appropriate	68

Project 3 Picture story

Lower intermediate and above 8–13

| Description of the project | | 69 |
| Language and skills grid | | 70 |

Activity — *Time (minutes)*

3.1	Jumbled cartoons	30	72
3.2	Tell me a story	45	73
3.3	Guess the story	60	74
3.4	Story lucky dip	60	76

Intermediate and above 11–13

3.5	Story types	60	77
3.6	Creating a story	90	81
3.7	Behind the scenes	60	83
3.8	Making the storyboard	60–90	85
3.9	Taking pictures	60–90	86
3.10	Creating the photo story	60	88

Project 4 Music

Elementary and above 11–13

| Description of the project | | 91 |
| Language and skills grid | | 92 |

Activity — *Time (minutes)*

4.1	Design a CD or cassette cover	60	94
4.2	Invent a pop band	60	96
4.3	A day in the life of a pop star	60	98

4.4	Design an outfit for a	60	100
4.5	Fashion show	60	101
4.6	Making music	60	102
4.7	Music from around the world	60	103
4.8	Write a song	60	105
4.9	Mystery band	45	107
4.10	The ELMAs—The English Language Music Awards	90	109
4.11	Make a fanzine	As appropriate	111

Project 5 Fantasy island

Intermediate and above 12–14

Description of the project		113
Language and skills grid		114
Activity	*Time (minutes)*	
5.1	Map your island!	90	116
5.2	Fly the flag	30–40	117
5.3	Fantasy creatures	60	119
5.4	Ideal homes	30–40	120
5.5	Celebrity guests	30	121
5.6	Tour of the island	45–60	122
5.7	Making money	60	124
5.8	Fantasy holidays	60	125
5.9	Elect a president	90	126
5.10	Fantasy island poetry book	60–90	130
5.11	Island news	60	133

Photocopiable worksheets	135
Further reading	149
Indexes	153
Questionnaire	154

The author and series editor

Diane Phillips trained as a teacher and then went on to do her MA and PhD in Applied Linguistics. She has worked as a teacher, teacher trainer, and Director of Studies at various schools throughout the world. She has recently been involved in the formulation of guidelines for EAQUALS inspection of centres which hold courses for young learners. She is currently working as the Head of Young Learners' and Offsite Courses at the Bell Educational Trust, a Senior Assessor for the UCLES DTEFLA/DELTA scheme, and is a member of a working party on awards for teachers of young learners: CELTYL and DELTYL. She has been involved in the writing of several other publications, including, *Teaching Practice Handbook* (with Gower and Walters, Heinemann 1995), and 'Teacher Training: Observation and Feedback' (in *Learning to Train: Perspectives on the Development of Language Teacher Trainers*, edited by Ian McGrath, Prentice Hall 1997).

Sarah Burwood has a BA Honours degree and an RSA DTEFLA. She has worked as a teacher and teacher trainer in Italy. She has also been Director of Offsite Courses, Youth Programmes Co-ordinator, and Course Director for the Studio School of English in Cambridge. Until recently, she was an Academic Manager for Young Learners courses at the Bell Educational Trust in Saffron Walden, and is currently working as a ESL/EFL teacher and freelance teacher trainer in Vancouver.

Helen Dunford has an MA in Applied Linguistics, a PGCE in TESOL, and an RSA DTEFLA. She has over eighteen years of teaching experience, including five years in primary English at the Ecole Française de Londres and a bilingual junior school in Lyon. She has worked as a teacher of young learners at The British Council in Naples, and co-ordinated training courses for teachers in Argentina, Colombia and Bulgaria. Until 1997 she was Head of Studies of the Young Learners Department of the Bell Educational Trust in Saffron Walden. She is currently working as Academic Director of International House, Portland, Santa Monica and San Francisco.

Alan Maley worked for The British Council from 1962 to 1988, serving as English Language Officer in Yugoslavia, Ghana, Italy, France, and China, and as Regional Representative for The British Council in South India (Madras). From 1988 to 1993 he was Director-General of the Bell Educational Trust, Cambridge. From

1993 to 1998 he was Senior Fellow in the Department of English Language and Literature of the National University of Singapore. He is currently a freelance consultant. He is also Dean of the Institute of English Language Education, and Director of the graduate English Programme at Assumption University in Bangkok. He wrote *Quartet* (with Françoise Grellet and Wim Welsing, OUP 1982), and *Literature*, in this series (with Alan Duff, OUP 1990). He has also written *Beyond Words*, *Sounds Interesting*, *Sounds Intriguing*, *Words*, *Variations on a Theme*, and *Drama Techniques in Language Learning* (all with Alan Duff), *The Mind's Eye* (with Françoise Grellet and Alan Duff), *Learning to Listen* and *Poem into Poem* (with Sandra Moulding). He is also Series Editor for the New Perspectives and Oxford Supplementary Skills series.

Foreword

The demand for materials suitable for use with young learners continues to grow. Many of the materials currently available offer sets of activities which the teacher can draw upon to supplement regular course materials, or to introduce novelty.

This book differs from such materials in offering coherently organized projects which can engage the learner over a period of time. Each project is broken down into a set of self-contained units, which can be used separately or built up sequentially into a final project outcome.

The advantages of this approach are:

- that the projects aim to draw upon the 'whole child', that is to say, all aspects of children's life, not simply their linguistic competence. This enables them to relate what they know from their own lives to a concrete problem worked through in the target language.

- that the projects encourage, even demand, that learners take a greater responsibility for their own learning than is often the case with more conventional materials. As such, they are in line with current thinking on 'learner independence'.

- that they allow learners with different levels of competence to co-operate on an equal basis in the completion of the tasks the project requires. This goes some way to solving the problems of mixed-ability classes.

- that the level of personal involvement by learners is consequently higher, which tends to enhance their motivation for continuing learning.

The authors have drawn upon their long experience of using a project-centred approach with young learners. What they offer here is a distillation of this experience. The units are clearly organized and laid out so that even a teacher unfamiliar with the approach can implement it.

For any teacher, experienced or not, who is looking for a set of well-organized project frameworks, this book will be an essential guide. We hope it will serve as a springboard for teachers to develop their own projects.

Alan Maley

Introduction

Who is this book for?

Young learners

The projects described in this book are designed for children of primary and early secondary school age, from five to fourteen. All the ideas and activities have been devised, or developed and tried out, by practising teachers; they have been used and evaluated with a wide range of nationalities, in both monolingual and multilingual groups of various sizes.

Children of the same age vary in terms of their maturity, intelligence, cultural, and home background. So, although an age range is recommended for each activity, you, the classroom teacher, are the best person to judge whether the topic and activities of the project are of interest to, and within the capabilities of, your pupils.

Through project work in their English class, the children will be encouraged to develop their intellectual, motor (physical), and social skills. However, they should not be expected to do tasks in a second or foreign language that they could not attempt in their first language. Teachers of English should be aware, for example, of the literacy skills that the children have in their first language and, especially for the very young children, how much opportunity they have had to practise such motor skills as cutting, folding, colouring, and so on.

Teachers

You will find the activities in this book useful if you are a teacher:
- in a primary school, where English language tuition is included in the curriculum
- in a private language school, and you wish to integrate motivating and challenging activities and materials into a standard coursebook-based curriculum
- of children on an intensive course, in English-speaking countries in the summer
- in a UK school or an English medium school, and you wish to help pupils bridge the gap from the specialized English as a Foreign Language classes to the mainstream classes.

Why project work?

The project is an ideal vehicle for teaching primary school children for a number of reasons.

It is an integrated unit of work

A project is a recognizable unit of work with a beginning, middle, and end. Through a series of worthwhile activities, which are linked to form a tangible end-product, the children can gain a real sense of achievement. At the successful completion of the project, both teacher and pupils have something they can be proud of, to show to parents and to others in the school as an indication of the progress they have made.

It educates the whole child

A project involves the development of the whole child, rather than focusing narrowly on teaching language. Within the framework of a project can be included the full range of skills that children are developing in their other classes and during their time out of school:

- the **intellectual** skills of describing, drawing conclusions, using the imagination, hypothesizing, reading, and planning
- the **physical/motor** skills of colouring, painting, cutting, folding, gluing, and writing
- the **social** skills of sharing, co-operating, making decisions together, and appreciating how individual contributions can make a successful whole
- **learner independence** skills such as making responsible choices, deciding how to complete tasks, getting information, trying things out, and evaluating results.

This approach encourages **emotional** and **personal** development. Wherever possible, children are given an opportunity to produce work which is personal and individual, which reflects their ideas, tastes, and interests; they are encouraged to express their feelings, and their opinions are sought and valued.

Project work gives the children an opportunity to bring their knowledge of the world into the classroom, and to extend their general knowledge of the topic under focus. Projects can encompass a wide range of topics and often draw on knowledge gained from other subjects in the curriculum.

It integrates language knowledge and skills

The project is a prime example of **experiential learning**. Language introduced and practised within a project is directly related to the task in hand; the children use the language that is needed for the successful completion of the activity. A project introduces and practises language, and integrates language skills, in a natural way. The language aims, for the project as a whole and for each activity, should be clear in the teacher's mind but do not always need to be made explicit to the children. Younger learners are concerned with what they can achieve through language: they see language as a means to an end, rather than as a body of knowledge to be learned.

There is evidence that, through repeated exposure, patterns of a second language can be internalized by young children in much the same way as they are with the first language. As they get older, children often take a more analytical approach and, as part of their development as independent learners, can be helped to recognize and label grammatical and lexical patterns. This awareness can be built into project work when appropriate.

It encourages learner independence

Successful experiential learning depends on the students also learning skills that will eventually enable them to continue their learning independently of the teacher. Project work helps children make choices, and take responsibility for their own work. It is also through project work that children can start developing the research and study skills that they need in order to progress in all the subjects within the curriculum in their secondary and further education.

It caters for mixed-ability classes

Projects can cater for classes in which there are children with a range of abilities, needs, and interests. Within class project work, there are often opportunities for different children to make different contributions, depending on their capabilities. If individual contributions are valued, the children's confidence is boosted, they feel positive about their English classes, and they are motivated to continue to do well.

A project allows for flexibility within the curriculum

Projects can be used either as a supplement, or complement, to the programme which is set by the school, or as the main structure round which the syllabus is designed. None of the projects in this book take more than twenty hours to complete (if all the activities are completed and time is spent on setting up and evaluating the project, as part of the learner training process). They are therefore ideal if you have a short time in which to achieve results, for example:

- on a short intensive course such as a three-week summer school
- where you may only see pupils for a few hours each week and not much time can be devoted to the project within the timetable of the school year.

How to use this book

How the book is organized

There are five projects in the book. The projects are graded in terms of the topic, the age group, the level of the language, and the difficulty of the tasks—the projects most suitable for younger children are at the beginning of the book, and those designed for older pupils, with a higher-level of English, are at the end of the book.

Number	Title	Level	Age Group
1	Let's have a party!	Beginner and above	5–9
2	Block of flats	Elementary and above	8–11
3	Picture story part one 3.1–3.4	Lower-intermediate and above, or as a set of introductory activities to part two	8–13
	Picture story part two 3.5–3.10	Intermediate and above	11–13
4	Music	Elementary and above	11–13
5	Fantasy island	Intermediate and above	12–14

Each project consists of ten to twelve activities, which link to achieve the overall aims of the project.

At the beginning of each project there is a description of the project, a list of the main products of each activity, and a language and skills grid which sets out:
- the language which arises in the project—grammar and vocabulary
- the skills practised—the language skills of reading, writing, listening, and speaking; the motor skills of cutting and drawing, and so on.

How each activity is organized

For each separate activity there is indicated: the minimum level necessary to do the activities in the project (beginner, elementary, lower-intermediate, intermediate, upper-intermediate); the age group; an approximate time within which the activity can be completed; a brief description setting out the aim of the activity; the language which arises; the materials needed; the preparation you, the teacher, need to do; step-by-step instructions, illustrated by diagrams; variations; any follow-up activities; comments about how the activity can be adapted or linked with other activities.

Most of the activities are complete in themselves. So, you can select activities to use with your class, even if you do not have time to complete all the activities that make up the project.

Planning the project

Integrating the project into the curriculum

The projects in this book have been planned to incorporate language points, vocabulary items, and skills which are suitable for children of a particular age and level. Each activity integrates grammar and vocabulary, and by the end of each project a balance of skills has been achieved.

When choosing one of the projects to do with your class, you will have to look carefully at the language (grammar and vocabulary) required for each activity, and the order in which it is introduced. You need to assess to what extent the project relates to work your class has already done, and how the language needs of your individual pupils, and of the group as a whole, can be met.

In some cases, the project may have to fit in with a syllabus (a checklist of grammar and vocabulary items) which has been designated for your class.

You may decide to select certain activities from a project, rather than do every activity in the order suggested. If you do this, you will need to make sure that the children understand any language essential for the selected activity which is introduced in earlier activities in the project.

In some of the projects, particularly the ones designed for students at intermediate level and above, you may find that your students are not yet familiar with some of the language which is revised and practised. In this case, you may need to spend time introducing a grammar point or a set of vocabulary items in a separate lesson, before the activity can be tackled. There may also be language points that are required for the class syllabus which is not included in the project. In this case, you will have to add activities which introduce and practise these points. If possible, try to select or create activities which are related to the overall theme of the project.

In other words, you need to integrate project work with other work that you do with your class, supplementing or omitting where necessary.

Planning a new project

If, after successfully completing the projects in this book, *you* wish to plan a project around a topic that you know to be of interest to your class, you may find it useful to start by drawing up a project web. This is the web that was used for planning Project 1: 'Let's have a party!'.

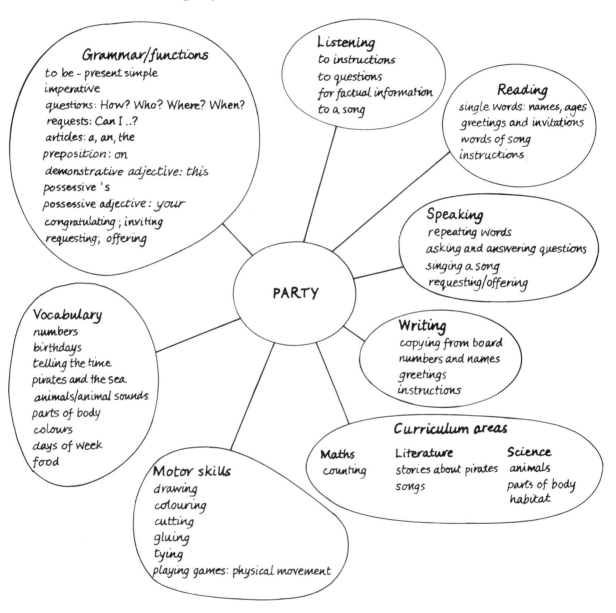

We find the best way to start is to think of the end-product (a model, a video, a wall display, a booklet, and so on) you wish to achieve, and the activities that will lead to successful completion of this end-product. Under each of the headings on the web, make a note of grammar points, functions, vocabulary areas, and skills that are needed for each activity.

Next, evaluate whether the items you have noted are appropriate for the level of the children. Is there a good balance of skills? Are there useful links with the children's other school subjects? You may need to omit one or two of the activities you first thought of if they require language or skills which are too advanced for the class. On the other hand, you may need to introduce some activities in order to give practice in a particular language area or skill which you want to include in the work of the class, or which is part of a required syllabus.

Look carefully at the order of the activities you plan to do. Do you introduce new language in a logical manner? Do the activities that come later in the project recycle language introduced in earlier activities?

Planning the end-product

The end-product of the project is important and should be carefully planned for. However, you should not give the product so much importance that you neglect the process. It is better to have a small amount of high quality work than a mass of badly presented, poor quality stuff. Most importantly it should be the *children's* work, not the teacher's, which is admired. In general, do not be over ambitious in what you can achieve in the time available, and leave plenty of time for preparing the final display.

Projects can have a range of different end-products, for example: a poster display, a three-dimensional model, an exhibition, a magazine or newspaper, a report, a video or audio cassette, or an event such as a party or a show. When planning your project you have to decide:

– how to store on-going work which is being collected to make up the final end-product
– how the project is going to be displayed.

If you have regular use of a classroom, a lot of work such as posters, pictures, stories, charts, maps, reports, and so on can be displayed on the walls. If the end-product takes the form of an exhibition, the display is built up as the project progresses. If you cannot leave work in the classroom, you may need to use portfolios or boxes for the storage of the things the children have made.

However you decide to show off the project to the 'public', the children should also have a record of the work they have done for and around the project. This usually takes the form of a file or folder into which work for the project is put, together with project plans or timetables, objectives for the project, written grammar exercises, vocabulary lists, homework tasks, tests, reports on progress, and evaluation sheets. The children will need help in keeping their files tidy and organizing their work under separate headings. The files can be shown to parents at the end of the course or term and there can be a prize for the best-presented file.

Presentation of the project

When presenting the project to others you have to decide:

Who? To parents, friends, other teachers, pupils in the school, the wider public?

Where? In the classroom, the school hall, a theatre, outdoors, in a video room?

How? A display can be staged as for the opening, or preview, of an new art exhibition with guests being sent invitation cards, drinks and nibbles provided, and talks from the 'artists'.
A video can be treated as a film at the cinema with popcorn and ice-cream for the 'audience'.
An event, such as a party or show, will involve invitation cards or programmes, and refreshments.
You and your students can devise a questionnaire or 'trail' for the visitors who are viewing the project display, with a prize for the person who finds out the most information.

Introducing project work to the parents

If you are introducing project work for the first time in your class you may want to have a meeting with parents to explain the rationale for learning language in this way. You can outline the sort of activities the children will be doing in class; the language they will be learning; the skills to be practised; the end-product(s) to be achieved. You can also explain how the children's progress will be evaluated and how you will inform them of their own child's performance and progress. If you can get parents involved from the start they will be supportive of your and the children's efforts.

Give parents a timetable of the activities and give plenty of notice of any project display or event that they will be invited to. You may also be able to enlist their help in providing some of the materials needed for the activities: pictures and photographs, old magazines, cooking ingredients, materials for decoration, maps, and so on.

Introducing the project to the children

You will certainly want to spend time at the beginning of the course or term talking about the project with the children. How you do this will depend on the age of the children in your group. Very young children will not question your methods, whilst older students, perhaps used to other ways of language learning, will welcome a more thorough explanation and rationale. This is the first step in raising the students' awareness of the value of learning a language in this way and the part they have in making it work. It is important that you make the children feel that their interests are genuinely reflected in the detailed planning.

During the introduction stage, again depending on the age of the children, you can discuss the end-product(s), the language they will be learning, the skills they will be practising, the way their progress will be monitored and assessed, the choices they will have. A timetable, plan of work, or checklist of objectives can be drawn up and ticked off as the project progresses. For young children this can be a series of pictures, in calendar format.

In low-level monolingual groups, the introduction can be done in the children's first language. With higher-level students the introduction, if carefully planned, can be an ideal opportunity for authentic language use.

Negotiation and choice

With all but the very young children, opportunity should be given for the students to determine certain aspects of the project. A number of choices can be presented to them for discussion at the beginning of the project and at stages throughout the project. Answers to these (and other) questions can be discussed and decided:

– Should everyone do all aspects of the project, or would it be better to allocate certain tasks to certain students?
– To what extent can they take responsibility for finding information and providing materials, and so on?
– How much can they do outside of class time?
– How do they wish to make best use of the teacher's time? For example, can they get on with work so that the teacher can conduct individual tutorials?
– How do they wish to display their work at the end of the project?

In addition to these bigger decisions, choices are built into all the projects in the book, and there are opportunities for the children to personalize their work. Any decisions that the children make will help foster a feeling of ownership of and responsibility for the project and increase their motivation.

Managing the project

If you are new to project work you may be concerned about classroom management and discipline. A group of children doing project work can appear to be disorganized and noisy. With artwork involved it can also be messy! If groups of children are engaged on different tasks it is difficult to monitor and assist more than one group at a time.

The following tips may help:

– introduce the project carefully (see *Introducing the project to the children*), so the children know what to expect and what behaviour is permissible

- establish the 'rules' (for example, *always wear an apron when painting*)
- to introduce project work, first choose an activity in which there is a lot of whole-class work before one in which different groups do different tasks
- plan your lessons very carefully so that you know exactly what you want the children to do at each stage; plan the work for individual groups if necessary
- have all your materials prepared and laid out in the order in which you need them; you may need different 'packs' of materials for different groups
- if possible arrange the furniture and prepare the board before the children come into the classroom; write up a schedule—the 'Activities for the Day', any instructions, the names of children in particular groups, vocabulary items, and so on
- give very clear instructions (in the mother tongue if necessary) and check that the children know what they have to do for their individual/group tasks before setting them off
- when the children are working individually/in groups, monitor to make sure they are all working satisfactorily; have a system so that the children can ask you for help in an orderly way, for example, by putting up their hands
- don't be concerned if they chatter when doing creative tasks—painting, model-making, and so on. Even if they speak in their mother tongue they are developing their social skills, and the chat adds to the enjoyment of the activity
- plan time at the end of the lesson when materials are packed away and the whole class comes together quietly; when you can sum up what has been achieved and make sure the children know about any homework or preparation they have to do for the next lesson.

Evaluation of project work and measuring progress

When planning project work it is important to allocate time for the evaluation of both the process (the doing) and the product (the tangible results). You need to build in slots within the timetable in which you and the children can look back at *what* you have done, *why* you did it, and at *how successful* you have been. There can be regular review lessons after a unit of work, at the end of each week or month and, of course, at the end of the project, depending on how often you see your class and how much time you have with them. How often you can find time for individual feedback will also depend on your situation.

Evaluation is valuable for the teacher and for the students. It helps you adapt your materials and methods, both during the project, and when planning future projects. Ongoing evaluation raises the children's awareness of how they learn and is part of the important process of helping them become more independent learners.

Evaluation is also essential in helping children and their parents appreciate the achievements of the class, of individual children in the group, and the progress that has been made. This is particularly important where project work is new and is being used instead of a coursebook-based syllabus. When parents and children are used to assessing progress by how much of the coursebook has been completed, it takes care and attention on the part of the teacher to help them become aware of the value of project work.

As when introducing and negotiating the project, in low-level monolingual groups the evaluation activities can be done in the children's first language. However, discussion in English wherever possible provides further opportunity to use English in an authentic way and is even possible with low-level multilingual groups if carefully structured (see the activities below). You may choose to conduct some of the evaluation tasks in the children's first language and some in English, depending on the nature of the activity.

Project plan and objectives

Having a plan of what is to be achieved in the project which can be referred to throughout the course or term is a useful way of raising the children's awareness of the project objectives and of reminding them of the progress they have made. Each student can have a copy of the negotiated plan in their files. The plan can also be in the form of a wall poster on which the different elements of the project are charted. For older children a plan of work can note the grammatical, functional, lexical, and skills objectives of the project in list or table form. Or, a project web can serve as a graphic reminder of the work to be done. As the project progresses the objectives can be evaluated and ticked off. For younger children the plan can be in the form of a calendar—with a picture for each day depicting the activity to be achieved. As each activity is completed the picture can be ticked off.

Project diary or log

Higher-level students can keep track of where they are up to in the project by keeping a class diary or log of what the class has achieved. Entries in the log can be made after whole-class discussion, by groups if they are working on different aspects of the project, or by individual students taking responsibility in turn.

Activities for reviewing and evaluating

Preference charts

There are a variety of ways the children can say whether they liked/didn't like an activity, whether they found it interesting or useful, or if they would like more or less of a particular type of activity. For example, by means of a bar chart:

This week we:

sang a song about a spider   made a poster
     made a birthday card   read a story about a hungry caterpillar
          played 'Simon Says'
Write the activity you liked best (1), the activity you liked next (2), etc.

| 1 |
| 2 |
| 3 |
| 4 |
| 5 |

Or by means of a list that each student makes up for himself/herself, to be discussed in the class or individually with the teacher. For example:

This week's work	
Useful activities for me	**Not so useful**
Listening to the song on cassette	Playing the game
Making up a questionnaire	Doing the grammar exercise
Reading the magazine article	

Answering 'yes/no' questions about the way they like to learn can be used to evaluate the project approach in general and help children become aware of their own preferred strategies. Again, the individual charts can be filled in then discussed in groups, in class, or individually with you.

How I like to learn	Yes or *No*?
I like listening to music when I am working.	Yes
When you're reading a story it is a good idea to look up every word you don't know in the dictionary.	No
It doesn't matter if you make mistakes. It's more important to speak.	Yes
I like playing games.	Sometimes
I like making things.	Yes
I like acting.	No
If you want to remember words you must study them.	Yes

Class review and evaluation

Evaluation and review of work is built into many of the activities included in the projects. Example tasks include:

- looking at and reviewing each other's finished work
- selecting the best examples from the different groups for inclusion in the class magazine or for a wall display
- awarding prizes for the best contributions
- giving short presentations about the work different groups have done
- showing a video clip or presenting an audio recording
- presenting a role play or sketch.

In all these tasks the children are evaluating their work and that of others. You can help this process by providing structured feedback tasks, for example:

Evaluation task			
For each of the poster displays make comments in the boxes:			
People in the group	Title of poster	Three things I particularly liked	One suggestion for improvement
1			
2			
3			
4			

Photocopiable © Oxford University Press

When the children are used to doing evaluation tasks you can even ask them to decide how they would like to get feedback from you and the other students in the class. They can make up their own evaluation task or questionnaire.

Assessing individual achievement

Reports on individual progress

Older students can be asked to give a personal report on 'work in progress'—what they have enjoyed/didn't like, what they have learned, found easy/difficult, problems they are having with their research, interesting facts they have discovered. The report can be spoken or written and can be used as the basis for an individual tutorial with the teacher.

Younger children can be asked to write an individual log or diary of their project and their progress. You can provide a template for them to fill in.

PROJECT DIARY

Name: **Date:**

_____   _____

Today, I made/learned

_____

I spoke in English to

_____

I wrote

_____

One problem I had today

_____

Next, I'm going to

_____

Measuring progress

To a large extent the class end-product and each student's file constitute tangible proof of the work achieved. However, you should plan for 'milestones' along the way. It is important to help the children measure and appreciate their own progress, and also have that progress recognized.

One way of doing this is by means of checklists which cover the work of several units of work within the project. This is a checklist of a student who has just finished the first three units of Project 4 – Music:

Name: Sylvia Lee **Teacher:** Ms Grant	**Finished**	**Checked**
Objectives achieved	**Finished**	**Checked**
I can use the present simple and adjectives to describe people, for example: *Leonardo DiCaprio has short blond hair. He is quite tall.*	✔	RG
I know some ways of expressing *like* and *dislike*, for example: *I really love …, I can't stand…, I'm keen on …*	✔	RG
I know at least *21* words and expressions to do with music, for example: *a band, a hit record.*	✔	RG
I can use the past simple to talk about past events in somebody's life, for example: *The band Oasis met in 1992.*	✔	RG
I can ask questions to get information, for example: *What's the group called? When did they have their first hit record?*	✔	RG
I have written a biography.	✔	RG
I know some adverbs of frequency, for example: *usually, always, sometimes, every day.*	✔	RG
I have written and illustrated *'A day in the life of Peppy Grunge'.*	✔	RG
I can tell the time in English.	✔	RG
I have read an English book called *'The Beatles'.*	✔	RG
I used the Picture Dictionary.	✔	RG
I completed my homework sheet.	✔	RG
I did a spelling test and got *18/20*	✔	RG

Teacher assessment

There is a danger with project work that the contribution and progress of individual children may not be recorded by you, the teacher, and that you cannot give a detailed assessment of each child to the parents. In order to be able to keep track of each child in your class a record grid of the type shown below is recommended. A sheet is kept for each child, which you fill in on a regular basis, preferably at the end of each lesson. Comments can be included, and even a simple grading system. In this way, you will be able to assess how well individual pupils are doing within the class, you can give feedback to the students and to his/her parents when needed, and you will have information that can be used for more formal school reports.

GEORGE	Mon	Wed	Fri	Mon	Wed	Fri
participation	good	v. good – answered lots of ??	quiet today	fine	good – very keen	fine
cooperation	good – worked well in group	fine	fine	good – helped M	fine	good
task completion	good – finished quickly	fine	Test work 18/20	fine	slow – did not finish in time	finished task from Wed.
understanding	fine	did not understand use of Pres. perf. immed.	fine	fine	not sure	fine
homework	did not give in	gave in exercise	Exercise: 9/10		gave in story	Story: Grade A
finished projects		finished report	Report – v. good – Grade B			
books read				'The Stolen Necklace'		

Encouraging learner independence

The planning, choosing, and evaluating activities described above all encourage learner independence. They help the learners understand what they are doing in the classroom and why; they raise the children's awareness of which learning strategies work best for them, and they encourage them to take responsibility for their own work. Children also learn to appreciate the need for co-operation and the importance of individual contributions to the success of the whole project.

Project work, if well planned and set up, encourages the learners to work independently even when they are not being directly supervised by the teacher, and tasks can often be continued outside the classroom.

Study skills

Project work goes hand in hand with the development of study skills. Good study skills, of course, are not only useful when learning a language but for most subjects across the curriculum. The development of study skills helps the children become better and more autonomous all-round learners. While doing project work appropriate time should be planned to help the children learn and practise the following skills.

- **How to organize their files and notebooks.** Ways of organizing their work can be introduced to the children at the start of the project. However, they will need constant reminders whenever you give out a worksheet, ask the children to copy from the board, ask them to make a note of new vocabulary, give back some homework, and so on, until they get used to automatically recording and filing their work in an organized way.

- **How to record new grammar and vocabulary.** This can be focused upon whenever new language items arise from the project. At first the children will need guidelines from you, and a clear model to copy from the board. Give the children time to record the new language and help them store the information in the correct section of their files. Gradually, they will learn to record items of language they meet in the course of their work, even at times when you are not there to prompt them.

- **How to use dictionaries.** The introduction to dictionary work can be via picture dictionaries for young children. Gradually, they can be taught how to check the spelling, meaning, and pronunciation of words and expressions, in both translation and monolingual dictionaries. There are numerous opportunities to introduce dictionary work when doing reading or writing tasks.

- **How to use grammar reference books.** These are skills that can be introduced as the learners begin to understand the importance of grammatical patterns. You can help by familiarizing them with grammatical terminology—the parts of speech, the names of tenses, and so on, and by giving them grammar research tasks so that eventually they can use grammar reference books independently.

- **How to find information in reference books.** Project work relies on students eventually being able to do their own research. You can help the children make a start in acquiring these skills by bringing in a few reference books related to the topic of the project for them to look at. Give them practice in using the contents and index pages. More advanced learners can be helped to make use of the reference books to help them with their individual project work and eventually they can be encouraged to use libraries for research.

Project 1
Let's have a party!

Description of the project

In this project the children prepare for and have a party. The main vocabulary areas are parties, food and drink, animals, people, and parts of the body. The project display is the party itself, and friends and family are invited.

Main products of each activity

On completion of the project the class will have achieved/produced the following:

1.1 **Happy birthday**
A birthday card and badge

1.2 **Party game—pirates**
A party game about pirates and creatures of the seas
A group wall picture for display

1.3 **Party masks**
A party mask of an animal

1.4 **Party game—animal circle**
A party game about animals

1.5 **Party song—Old Macdonald had a zoo**
A party song about animals and the sounds they make

1.6 **Party game—pin the tail on the donkey**
A party game about animals and parts of the body

1.7 **Party crackers**
A party cracker with forfeits

1.8 **Party game—blind man's buff**
A party game about people

1.9 **Party food**
Party food (pretend)

1.10 **Party invitations**
A party invitation

1.11 **More party food**
Party food (real)

1.12 **Party time!**
A real party where the children play the games, sing the songs, eat the food, wear the masks, and pull the crackers.

Language and skills

Activity	Grammatical and functional	Vocabulary	Skills
1.1 **Happy birthday**	To be: *am, is, are* Questions with *how*: *How old are you?* Greetings for birthday cards	Numbers 1–10 *Birthday card, badge*	**Speaking and listening:** asking and answering questions about age **Writing:** copying from the board, writing on cards and badges **Other:** drawing; decorating
1.2 **Party game—pirates**	Instructions, some with imperative	Words about the sea: *ships* and *pirates*, sea creatures	**Listening:** to instructions **Speaking:** repeating words with actions **Reading and writing:** copying words **Other:** colouring pictures
1.3 **Party masks**	To be: *is* Demonstrative pronoun: *this* Articles: *a, an, the* Requests with *can*: *Can I have the zebra, please?*	Animals Parts of the animal's body: *face, whiskers, ears, nose, eyes*	**Listening:** to the teacher talking about the animals **Speaking:** asking for a picture of an animal **Other:** drawing; gluing
1.4 **Party game—animal circle**	To be: *I am (I'm)*— Questions with *who*: *Who are you?* Questions with *what*: *What colour is an elephant?* *Is it …? Yes, it is/ No, it isn't*	Animals: colours, and animal food	**Listening:** and responding to questions, for example, *What do snakes eat?* **Speaking:** asking and answering questions with Who …? What …? **Other:** drawing; colouring
1.5 **Party song—Old Macdonald had a zoo**	To be: *is* Demonstrative pronoun: *this* Indefinite articles: *a, an* Past tense (*had*), for exposure only	Animals and the sounds they make	**Listening** and remembering the words of the song **Speaking (singing):** the words of the song **Reading:** the words of the song **Writing:** copying the names and sounds of the animals on to the worksheet

1.6 **Party game—** **pin the tail on** **the donkey**	Questions with *where*: *Where is (Where's) …?* To be: *It is (It's) …* Preposition: *on* Possessive '*s*'	Animals Parts of animal's body: *nose, tail, trunk, ears*	**Speaking:** asking and answering questions **Writing:** copying the questions, answers, and labels for their pictures **Other:** painting or drawing; cutting out
1.7 **Party crackers**	Instructions, with the imperative: *Touch your* *nose.* Possessive adjective: *your*	Colours Animals and the noises they make Parts of the body *Sweet*	**Listening:** to instructions **Reading and writing:** instructions for forfeits – copying from the board **Other:** drawing; cutting; gluing; tying
1.8 **Party game—** **blind man's buff**	To be, question: *Is it?* Short answers: *Yes, it is/* *No, it isn't*		**Speaking and listening:** asking and answering questions **Other:** drawing or painting
1.9 **Party food**	Expressing likes and dislikes: *I like/don't like …* Making suggestions: *Let's …*	Party food and drink	**Speaking:** talking about likes and dislikes **Writing:** labels for food **Other:** drawing; colouring; cutting out
1.10 **Party** **invitations**	Questions with *When is* *(When's) …?* Telling the time Inviting	Days of the week	**Speaking:** asking and answering about days and times **Reading and writing:** party invitations **Other:** drawing or colouring in
1.11 **More party** **food**	Requesting and offering food and drink: *Can I* *have …? Would you* *like …?* *Please* and *Thank you*	Party food and drink Cooking utensils	**Speaking:** asking for and offering food and drink at a party **Listening:** to instructions **Other:** decorating a cake
1.12 **Party time!**	Use of any/all language introduced throughout the project	Vocabulary learned throughout the project	**Speaking and listening:** using the language they have learned to play the games, sing the songs, and to ask for and offer food and drink

1.1 Happy birthday

LEVEL	**Beginner and above**
AGE GROUP	5–9
TIME	**30 minutes**
DESCRIPTION	The children ask and answer questions about their age. They make a birthday card and badge for their teddy bears or, if they are older, for a famous cartoon character.
LANGUAGE	To be—*am*; *How old are you?* Numbers 1–10; greetings on birthday cards.
SKILLS	Drawing, decorating, and writing in cards.
MATERIALS	Card or thick paper; coloured pens; glitter and glue; safety pins and strong sticky tape; some old birthday cards for demonstration. The children each bring in a teddy bear or soft toy, or a picture of their favourite cartoon character.

PREPARATION

1 Make the badges by cutting out circles of card. Make one for each child's teddy bear. **Do not** stick the safety pins on at this stage.

2 Cut rectangles out of card. Fold the rectangle in half to make a card for each child.

IN CLASS

1 Revise numbers 1 to 10.

2 Introduce the question *How old are you?*, and the answer, *I'm (6)*. You could have a series of pictures of children, cartoon characters, or animals aged from 4 to 10, with a speech bubble from each saying *I'm 5*, *I'm 6*, and so on. Practise reading the bubbles and saying the short sentences together as a class.

3 Go around the class asking *How old are you?* with each child answering in turn.

4 Practise saying the question together, concentrating on pronunciation and intonation.

5 Go around the class—one child asks the question, the second child answers, then asks a third child, and so on, until all the children have asked and answered the question.

6 Give out the ready-made blank badges. Write on the board *I am 7*

Choose a number which is the most common age of the children in the class.

7 Tell the children to imagine that it is their teddy bear's or favourite cartoon character's birthday. Tell them that they are going to make a badge. The children choose the age that they want their teddies or characters to be, and copy the words on to the badges.

8 When the children have finished writing on their badges, attach a safety pin to the back. The children can save their badges to put on their toys, or attach them to the birthday cards they make.

9 Tell the children to walk around the room with their teddies, or pretend to be their favourite cartoon character. They should find out the age of three other toys or characters by asking *How old are you?*, and answering *I'm ...* .

10 Make the birthday cards. Draw a rectangle (on the board) for the front of the card. Write on the rectangle:

11 Give each child a piece of folded card. Tell them to copy the words on to their card. They then draw a picture in the centre of their card, and/or decorate it with glitter, and so on. You can suggest suitable pictures, for example, balloons or a birthday cake with candles. The picture can be drawn for homework if you wish. For children who can't write, you can give out the cards with the words already written on them.

12 Write on the board:

> *To ...*
> *With love from ...*

13 Tell the children to copy the words into their cards and fill in the age of the person, teddy, cartoon character, or friend they'd like to send it to (or give out the cards with these words already written in).

14 Show the children where to write the name of the person receiving the card, and their own name.

15 Older children can write a greeting inside the card. Make suggestions, for example, *Many Happy Returns! Have a good day!*

16 The cards can be displayed on the wall, or given to someone on their birthday.

FOLLOW-UP

1 Teach the children to sing the song 'Happy birthday to you', in preparation for the party.

Happy birthday to you

2 The teddy bears can accompany the children to the end of class party and have a 'teddy bears' picnic'.

1.2 Party game—pirates

LEVEL

Beginner and above

AGE GROUP

5–9

TIME

30 minutes (plus 60 minutes to make a pirate wall picture)

DESCRIPTION

The children learn the words and the rules, and play a party game.

LANGUAGE

Vocabulary about the sea, for example, *boat* and *pirate*; writing your name.

SKILLS

Listening to instructions; colouring pictures; copying from the board.

MATERIALS

Photocopiable Worksheet 1.2, or pictures from magazines; coloured pens; large sheets of paper; paints; large sheets of blue paper to make a sea picture to cover a wall.

PREPARATION

If possible, push the furniture to the side of the room so that the children can move around.

IN CLASS

1 Introduce and practise saying the words using the pictures: *ship, pirate(s), lifeboat(s), captain, crab, jellyfish, shark,* and any other sea animals you want to use.

2 Using the pictures and mime, teach the instructions and the actions that go with them.

Words	Actions
Swim	*make swimming movements*
Pirates	*stand on one leg and cover one eye*
All aboard	*come to the centre of the room which is the pirate's ship*
Captain's coming	*salute*
Lifeboats	*sit down and row a boat*
Jellyfish	*shake the body*
Crabs	*with your hands on the floor walk sideways*
Shark	*find a friend, hug them, and shout* Help!

3 **a** Start by saying *swim* – the children make swimming movements and move around the room.
  b Say *pirates* – the children do the pirate action.
  c Say *swim* – the children do the swimming action.
  d Choose another word and the children do the actions, and so on.
  e Between each of the actions say *swim* and let the children move.

4 Put your pictures on the board, elicit the words, and write them under the pictures: *a ship, a pirate, a crab, a shark, a jellyfish, a lifeboat*. Practise saying the words and let the children copy from the board, drawing their own pictures above the words.

VARIATION

Older children with a higher level of English can play a more difficult variation of the game:

a Stand the children in a circle.

b Choose the names of three or four fish, for example: *cod, herring, plaice*, and *trout*. Stick labels with fish names on the children.

c When you call out *All the fish in the sea* they must **all** do the actions. If you say, *Cod—Captain's coming*, only the cod salute while the others continue to do the previous action.

Other examples of instructions and actions:
All the fish in the sea—swim—all the children move around the room swimming.
Pirates—all the children do the pirate action.
Herrings—jellyfish—only the herrings shake while the others continue to be pirates.
The fish teams can lose a point if someone makes a mistake with the actions.

FOLLOW-UP

Sea wall picture
a In pairs or individually, the children choose what they would like to draw and paint—a shark, a jellyfish, and so on—there should be at least one pirate ship with some pirates and lots of sea creatures. The children draw and paint their pictures on to large sheets of paper. When the pictures are dry, the children cut them out.

b While they are busy painting, stick up some blue paper on the wall to make a seascape wall frieze. Sketch in some details with chalk, for example, the waves and where the sea bottom and sand are (see picture below as an example).

c As the children are waiting for their pictures to dry, they can add details to the main wall frieze picture, for example, sand, seaweed, waves, shells, and seagulls. Introduce the words as they are needed. When the children's pictures are finished, the children decide where they would like to stick them on the group picture.

1.3   Party masks

LEVEL	**Beginner and above**
AGE GROUP	**5–9**
TIME	**45 minutes**

DESCRIPTION

The children make an animal mask that they can use later to play various party games.

LANGUAGE

This is a … ; *Can I have a … please?* animals; parts of an animal's body, for example: *face, whiskers,* and *ears.*

SKILLS

Drawing; gluing.

MATERIALS

Paper plates (see and study diagram for instructions to make masks); coloured paints; paper straws (for whiskers); coloured card; scissors; glue; Blu-Tak or sticky tape; pictures of animals.

PREPARATION

1 Collect as many pictures of different animals as possible. You will need enough different animals for each child in the class.

2 Write the names of the animals on separate strips of card.

3 Prepare paper plates for masks (see diagram and instructions).

IN CLASS

1 Teach/revise animals, *This is a monkey*, and so on, using the pictures.

2 Write the names of the animals on the board, stick a picture of each animal above its name, elicit the name, and practise saying it.

3 Rub off the names, point at the animals, and elicit the name from the children again. Write the words under the pictures on the board as the children say them.

4 Shuffle the animal name labels and give a label and a small piece of Blu-Tak or tape to each child (each child should have a different animal).

5 Stick the pictures of the animals on the walls around the room. Ask the children to stick their label under the correct animal picture. Check with the class that the animals are labelled correctly.

6 Either give each child a picture of an animal, or let the children choose a picture. Elicit the question, *Can I have the zebra, please?* Give out the plates for animal masks. The children colour or paint their masks using their animal pictures as a guide. Whiskers and ears can be added by using card or paper straws (see diagram). The children wear the masks tilted over their foreheads.

FOLLOW-UP

The children can make posters. They can glue a picture of their animal in the middle and draw pictures of where it lives, what it likes to eat, and so on, around the edge of the poster. Vocabulary and labels can be introduced as appropriate.

See *Young Learners* and *Drama with Children* for more masks.

1.4 Party game—animal circle

LEVEL

Beginner and above

AGE GROUP

5–9

TIME

45 minutes

DESCRIPTION

The children learn to ask and answer questions with *Who* and *What*, and remember the names of animals, what colour they are, and what they like to eat, in order to play the game.

LANGUAGE

Who are you? I'm a … ; questions starting with *What*, and their answers; *Is it a squirrel? Yes, it is/No, it isn't*; animals and animal colours and food.

SKILLS

Memory and playing games; listening and responding to questions; drawing; colouring.

MATERIALS

Small pictures of animals; a large bag to put all the pictures in.

PREPARATION

Collect as many pictures of animals as possible, there should be a different animal for each child in the class.

IN CLASS

1 Show the children the pictures of the animals and teach/elicit their names. Write a list of the animals on the board.

2 Ask the children what colour the animals are, for example:
What colour is an elephant? It's grey.
What colour is a giraffe? It's yellow and brown.
Teach/revise appropriate colour vocabulary.

3 Ask the children what the animals eat, for example:
What do elephants eat? Grass and leaves.
What do monkeys eat? Bananas.
Teach/revise appropriate food vocabulary.

4 Ask the questions and get the class to repeat them, focusing on pronunciation and intonation. Write some examples on the board. Ask the children to choose two animals, and write the questions and answers for their animals in their books, for example: *What colour is a shark? It's grey, What do sharks eat? Fish and people.* They can draw a picture of the animal, colour it the correct colour, and draw a picture of its food.

5 Put all the pictures in a bag. Ask a child to come out and pull a picture of an animal out of the bag. He/she mustn't show the picture to the class. Tell the other children to find out which animal it is by asking: *What colour is your animal? (It's brown), What does it eat? (Nuts), Is it a squirrel? (Yes, it is/No, it isn't).* Make sure each child has a turn to choose an animal, and ask and answer the questions. When each child has finished answering the questions, they take their picture of the animal and sit down.

6 Arrange the children's chairs in a circle with the seats facing inwards. Tell all the children to sit down holding their animal pictures in front of them. Ask each child the questions: *Who are you? (I'm a frog), What colour are you? (Green), What do you eat? (Flies).*

7 Explain that the children must remember which animal they are. Collect the animal pictures.

8 Ask one child to stand in the middle of the circle and remove one chair. Play the animal game:

a When you call out the names of two or more animals the children who are those animals must change places and the child in the centre of the circle must try to sit on an empty chair. The child who doesn't manage to sit in an empty chair is the next one in the middle. You can vary the way you call the animals out:
The zebra and the donkey change.
All the grey animals change.
All the animals that eat fish change.
All the black and white and yellow and brown animals change.
The elephant and the animal that eats bananas change.

b The child in the middle calls out the instructions when the class have practised the game with the teacher.

1.5 Party song—Old Macdonald had a zoo

LEVEL   **Beginner and above**

AGE GROUP   **5–9**

TIME   **30 minutes**

DESCRIPTION The children revise the names of the animals, learn the words of a song, and sing it.

LANGUAGE   To be—*is*; *this*; *a, an*; animals and the sounds they make.

SKILLS   Listening to, learning, and singing a song.

MATERIALS   The animal masks from 1.3 'Party masks'; a picture or drawing on the board, showing Old Macdonald and his zoo and cages containing some of the animals.

PREPARATION 1 Practise singing the song to the tune of 'Old Macdonald had a Farm' yourself.

2 Draw a picture of Old Macdonald and his zoo.

IN CLASS   1 The children wear the animals masks they made in activity 1.3. Revise *This is a monkey, This is a tiger*, and so on. Teach and practise the noise that each animal makes.

Animal	Noise	Animal	Noise
lion	*roar*	mouse	*squeak*
wolf	*howl*	pig	*oink*
cow	*moo*	frog	*croak*
zebra/horse	*neigh*	tiger	*roar*
sheep	*baa*	cat	*mew/meow*
birds	*tweet*	dog	*woof/bark*
donkey	*eeyore*	bear	*growl*
owl	*hoot*	monkey	*ooh ooh*
elephant	*trumpet*		

2 Show the picture of Old Macdonald and the zoo. Tell the children his name and teach/revise the word *zoo*.

3 Teach the children the song a few lines at a time:

Old Macdonald had a zoo (music traditional)

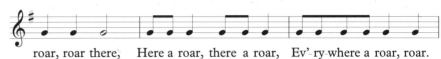

Old Macdonald had a zoo
E i, e i, o
And in that zoo he had a bear
E i, e i, o
With a growl, growl here …
    and so on.

4   The children stand in a circle, with you in the middle. At the line, *in that zoo he had a …* , choose a child and bring him or her into the centre of the circle. The child does the actions and makes the noises for the animal, while the other children continue to sing the song. The child in the middle chooses the next animal.

5   Repeat until all the children have had a turn.

VARIATION

If the children can read, you can give them the words of the song with blanks for the names and sounds of the animals. Copy the words on to sheets—one for each child. Let them read the words and learn to sing the song. They can illustrate the song with pictures of the different animals, and fill the blanks with the name and sound of their favourite one.

1.6   Party game—pin the tail on the donkey

LEVEL

Beginner and above

AGE GROUP

5–9

TIME

45 minutes

DESCRIPTION

The children learn the words and rules, and play the party game.

LANGUAGE

Where is (Where's) … ? It is (It's) … , on; possessive 's'; animals; parts of animal's body: *nose, tail, trunk,* and *ears.*

SKILLS

Painting or drawing; cutting out.

MATERIALS

One large sheet of paper for each child; card; paints, or large coloured pens; scissors; Blu-Tak; pictures of animals; scarves to use as blindfolds.

PREPARATION

1 Ask the children to bring in pictures of animals a few days before you do this activity or use the animal pictures from activity 1.3.

2 Either make a demonstration 'pin the tail' animal, or draw a large animal on the board and make a cardboard tail for this animal.

IN CLASS

1 Show the children your 'pin the tail' animal, with its tail. Explain that they are going to make their own animal for the game.

2 Show the children the animal pictures. Practise saying the names of the animals. Let them each choose an animal to draw. Make sure they each choose different animals.

3 The children draw or paint their animals. Make sure the pictures fill the large piece of paper. They also make a separate tail. Younger children may need some help with the cutting.

4 Using the pictures, teach/revise the different parts of the animal's body, for example: *tail, whiskers, trunk*, and *paws*. Teach the possessive 's', *The lion's nose, The donkey's ears*.

5 Stick your animal's tail on different parts of your picture and ask *Where's the tail?*, and elicit the answer *It's on the bear's nose*. Practise saying the questions and answers. Write the questions and some of the answers on the board. Teach *It's nowhere*, for when the tail misses the animal.

6 Show the children how to play using two volunteers at the front of the class. The children play the game in threes:

   a In turn, one child's picture is put on a board or the wall.

   b The child is blindfolded and turned around three times, while the other two children count *one, two, three*.

   c They then give him/her the tail with a piece of Blu-Tak on one end to stick it down.

   d The child sticks the tail somewhere on the picture and asks *Where's the tail?* The other two children then answer *It's on the elephant's leg*. The child tries again until he/she gets it in the right place.

FOLLOW-UP

1 The same day or in a later lesson (depending on how long the game takes), the children can label their pictures with the parts of the animal's body, choosing and copying the words from the board. Each child writes the question *Where's the tail?* on their picture, sticks their tail where they want it to go, and writes the answer, for example, *It's on the dog's ear*. The pictures can then be displayed on the wall.

2 The children can design fantasy animals with ears, noses, and tails in strange places. Show them some examples of fantasy creatures from books or modern art, for example, unicorns, mermaids, and Picasso portraits.

1.7 Party crackers

LEVEL	**Beginner and above**
AGE GROUP	**5–9**
TIME	**60 minutes**
DESCRIPTION	The children make party crackers with forfeits inside to pull at their party. The forfeits are instructions to do an action, or make a noise, for example, *Touch your toes.*
LANGUAGE	Imperatives; colours; parts of the body; animals and the noises they make.
SKILLS	Drawing; cutting; gluing; tying; copying from the board.
MATERIALS	Coloured card; crepe or tissue paper; ribbon or coloured string; cardboard tubes; magazines with coloured pictures for the children to cut out; scissors; glue; a bag of sweets; a selection of animal pictures.

PREPARATION

1 Prepare the templates for the tissue paper and card (see diagram and instructions on making the crackers).
2 Cut small strips of card to put inside the crackers, these will have the forfeits written on them.
3 Make a cracker to demonstrate in class.

IN CLASS

1 Teach/revise parts of the body. Say to the children: *touch your nose, touch your head*, and so on. Give each child a turn at giving instructions to the others. After the activity, write an example on the board:

   Touch your toes.

2 Teach/revise colours using instructions, for example: *touch something red, touch something blue.* After the activity, write an example on the board:

   Touch something green.

3 Revise names of animals using animal pictures, and practise animal noises, for example, *make a noise like a mouse, make a noise like an elephant.* After the activity, write an example on the board: *Make a noise like a lion.*

   Leave the example sentences on the board.

4 Explain that children are going to make crackers for a party, show them your example. Get one of the children to pull the cracker with you. Ask what is inside—show them the sweet inside and the forfeit, read the forfeit and get the children to do the forfeit.

5 Get the children to make their crackers:

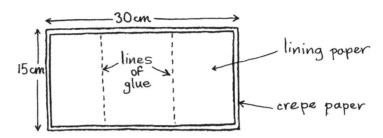

a Cut out a sheet of tissue paper and a sheet of cardboard, both 30 cm x 15 cm.

b Put two lines of glue on the piece of cardboard, as shown in the diagram, and stick the piece of tissue paper to the card.

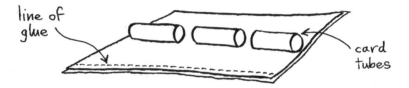

c Arrange three cardboard tubes (of equal length) on the tissue paper (see pictures).

d Apply glue along one edge of the paper and roll the paper carefully around the tubes.

e Write the forfeits: this will depend on the level of the children. You can let them write their own forfeits following the examples which you wrote on the board, or give out strips of card with the first half of the forfeit already written on them, *Touch your ...* , *Touch something ...* . Tell the children to complete them. Check to make sure their sentences are correct.

f Ask the children to illustrate their forfeits, for example, for *Make a noise like a mouse*, they draw a picture of a mouse.

g Tell the children to put a sweet and their forfeit inside the cracker.

h Wind some thread around the cracker in the spaces between the tubes, and tie tightly. Allow the glue to dry carefully and remove the outside tubes.

i The children can decorate the crackers by cutting out pictures from the magazine and sticking them on.

FOLLOW-UP

The crackers are pulled at the class party and the children do the forfeits inside their classmates' crackers.

VARIATION

You can choose more complex imperatives if the level of the class is higher, for example: *sing a song, jump up and down, or hop around the classroom.*

1.8   Party game—blind man's bluff

LEVEL	**Beginner and above**
AGE GROUP	5–9
TIME	**30 minutes**
DESCRIPTION	The children make posters of their friends and play the game 'blind man's buff'.
LANGUAGE	*Is it … ?, Yes, it is/No, it isn't.*
SKILLS	Drawing or painting; physical co-ordination.
MATERIALS	Large sheets of paper for portraits; paints or coloured pens; a scarf to use as a blindfold; some pictures of famous people that the children will recognize.
PREPARATION	Bring in pictures of familiar people or cartoon characters that the children will recognize, for example, Mickey Mouse and Winnie the Pooh.
IN CLASS	

1 Look at the pictures of the famous characters. Teach/revise: *Is this Tigger … ? Yes, it is/No, it isn't, this is …* using the pictures.
2 Put the children in pairs. The children draw or paint a picture of their partner. Under the picture the children write *This is … .*
3 Display the posters on the wall.
4 The class plays 'blind man's buff':
   a Stand the children in a circle.
   b Choose one child who comes into the middle of the circle.
   c Blindfold this child and turn him/her around three times (the children count as you do so).
   d The children in the circle move around until you say stop. You can play some music as they move. The children must stay silent.
   e The child in the blindfold moves out of the centre of the circle until he/she finds another child.
   f The child puts their hands on the other child's shoulders. He/she can touch their hair and try to guess who it is. He/she says: *Is it Sarah?* or *This is … .*
   g The other children respond: *Yes, it is/No, it isn't.*
   h If the child is wrong, he/she finds another person.
   i If he/she is correct, the child who she named becomes the 'blind man'.

1.9 Party food

LEVEL	**Beginner and above**
AGE GROUP	5–9
TIME	**60 minutes**
DESCRIPTION	The children learn to ask each other what kind of food they like. They choose what to eat and drink at their party and make cardboard party food and drink. This activity will prepare them for the next part of the project, making real party food.
LANGUAGE	Likes/dislikes; *Let's make* … ; party food and drink.
SKILLS	Drawing; colouring; cutting out cardboard food.
MATERIALS	Card or thick paper; crayons; coloured pens; scissors; labels for the items of food and drink; photocopies of Worksheet 1.9.
PREPARATION	1 Photocopy Worksheet 1.9.
	2 Bring in real items of food, or use pretend food or pictures.
IN CLASS	1 Show the items of party food and drink (real or pictures) and see how many the children can name. Practise saying the words.

2 Play a game where the children are each given a label which they have to put next to the correct item or picture. You can do this on a large table, or on the floor. If you use pictures, the labels can be stuck next to the picture on the wall.

3 Ask the children for the names of any other kinds of food or drink they like to have at parties. Provide the words in English and practise saying them. Write the words on the board—with a quick drawing if possible.

4 Give out the worksheets. Ask the children to write the name of each item under the pictures. If they are too young to write, you can write in the words before you photocopy the worksheet, and ask the children to colour the pictures. As they colour the pictures, go around the group and ask the children what each item is.

5 Teach *I like/I don't like* … , by selecting a few items and illustrating with facial expressions, and smiley/frowny faces. For example: *I like cake* (picture of a happy face), *I don't like milk* (picture of an unhappy face). It will be easier to demonstrate *I don't like* … , if you have a picture of something you know the children hate, like the ones in the pictures, cabbage, spinach, or soup! Practise saying the expressions using the real items/pictures of food and drink.

6 In pairs, the children can practise using the expressions by talking about the food and drink on their worksheets.

7 Explain to the children that they are going to make party food. Introduce and practise the expression: *Let's make … (a cake, some lemonade)*. Ask the children what they want to make, encouraging them to use the expression in their replies. Let each child choose one or two items to make.

8 Ask the children to paint their chosen food items. They can paint the pictures on to large paper plates, cut them out in different shapes, and create different effects using scrunched-up painted tissue paper, cut out cardboard shapes, and so on.

9 Let the children show their food and drink to the rest of the class. They can practise the language by mingling, showing what they have made to other children, and saying *I like … .*

VARIATION

1 You can introduce and practise the question: *Do you like …?* and the answers: *Yes, I do/No, I don't.*

2 With students who can already ask this question, you can also teach and practise: *What kind of food/drink do you like …?* and the answer, for example: *I like …, but I don't like … .* Model the sentences, then ask the children to practise in pairs or small groups.

1.10   Party invitations

LEVEL

Beginner and above

AGE GROUP

5–9

TIME

45 minutes

DESCRIPTION

The children talk about the days and time of events. They write an invitation for a party.

LANGUAGE

When is (When's) …? telling the time; days of the week; inviting people to a party.

SKILLS

Drawing or colouring in; decorating a card.

MATERIALS

Old invitations or a sample invitation to show the children; Card or thick paper; coloured pens; glitter, and so on, to decorate the cards; envelopes, if required.

PREPARATION

If you have low-level students, prepare invitation cards for them, as in step 6.

IN CLASS

1 Begin by teaching/revising the days of the week. Draw a week's calendar on the board.

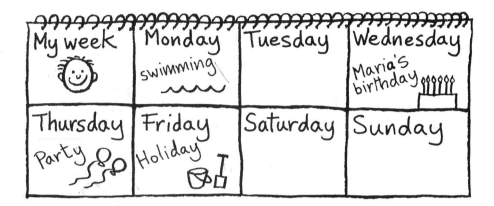

2 Introduce the question *When is (When's) …?* by writing some real events on days on the calendar. Practise saying the question, for example: *When's swimming? When's Maria's birthday?* and the reply: *It's on (Monday, Tuesday,* and so on).

3 Put *party* on the calendar, on the day you plan to have it, ask: *When's the party?* and elicit the answer.

4 Revise/teach the time (the hours only), for example: *It's 3 o'clock.* You could do this by drawing a clock on the board and changing the hands.

5 Write on the calendar, next to the word *party*, the time you plan to have the party, for example, *party at 4 o'clock.*

6 Show the example invitation card(s). Tell the children they are going to write their own cards to ask people to the party. Draw the invitation on the board:

7 Ask the children to look at the calendar, and suggest words to put in the spaces. Tell them to copy all the words on to their invitation cards. For low-level students, you could provide some

of the words on the cards (as above), and ask the children to write the words in the spaces. Outline pictures can be included on the card, for the children to colour in. Alternatively, the children can draw their own pictures and decorate their cards.

8 If anyone outside the class is going to be invited to the party, for example, another class, parents, or the headteacher, decide how the invitations are going to be sent. Help the children write the names of the party guests on the envelopes. If nobody from outside is coming, the children can exchange invitations with each other, or the invitations can be displayed on the classroom wall.

1.11   More party food

LEVEL	**Beginner and above**
AGE GROUP	**5–9**
TIME	**60 minutes**
DESCRIPTION	The children decorate small cakes to eat at the party. They practise asking for and offering food and drink at a party.
LANGUAGE	*Can I have some …? Would you like some …?*, *Please* and *Thank you.* Party food and drink; cooking utensils.
SKILLS	Decorating a cake; following instructions.
MATERIALS	Cardboard food prepared by the children and any pretend food used in 1.9 'Party food'; sponge cakes (one for each child); sugar, butter or margarine; water; sweets, sugar sprinkles, chocolate drops, glacé cherries, and so on for decoration; candles (optional); utensils—bowls, mixing spoons, small spoons, one set between three or four children.

PREPARATION

1 Make sure the children have aprons or old T-shirts to protect their clothes.

2 Find paper or cloths to protect desks/tables.

3 Try out the recipe for icing at home first!

IN CLASS

1 Using the cardboard food made by the children in 1.9 'Party food', introduce the request, *Can I have (a sandwich, some cola) please?*, the offer, *Would you like (a cake, some crisps)?*, and the replies *Yes, please/No, thank you.* Practise the language by letting the children offer and ask for the cardboard food and any pretend food you have (for example, empty bottles of cola).

2 Either make a large bowl of icing for the whole class, with each of the children taking turns to stir the mixture, or give a set of utensils and ingredients to each group of three or four children.

Give the following step-by-step instructions and demonstration for making a simple icing:

a Put two spoonfuls of soft butter or margarine in a bowl.
b Mix in one cup of icing sugar, a little at a time.
c If the mixture is dry, add a little water.
d Stir until smooth. (It should be soft enough to spread, without being runny.)

3 Let each child decorate his or her own cake with icing and other decorations. You can decorate one yourself first, to give them some ideas. For example: *Let's put some sweets here for eyes and a cherry to make the clown's nose.* Go around and help where necessary.

4 When they have finished, put all the cakes on display and let the children see each other's work. You can make appropriate comments: *That looks lovely/delicious!*

5 The children can now use the language they practised earlier to (pretend to) offer their cakes to guests: *Would you like a cake?*

6 The children can either eat their cakes immediately, or, if this activity is done the day or the morning before the party, the cakes can be stored and eaten at the party.

See *Very Young Learners* and *Young Learners* for ideas on making pizza faces and milk shakes for the party.

1.12 Party time!

LEVEL	**Beginner and above**
AGE GROUP	5–9
TIME	**60 minutes**
DESCRIPTION	All the previous activities are combined in the class party. The children wear the masks, play the games, sing the songs, pull the crackers, and eat the food with their invited guests.
LANGUAGE	Revision and practice of all the grammar and vocabulary from the previous eleven activities.
SKILLS	Playing games, and singing songs; having an 'English party'.

MATERIALS

You need to bring party food and drink, or ask each of the children/parents to bring something appropriate. You may decide to decorate the cakes just before the party, and save them to eat at the party. You can provide small prizes for the games.

PREPARATION

1 Send out the invitations.
2 Arrange for the food and drink to be brought. You may want to protect the furniture with paper or tablecloths.
3 Tell everyone in the school that you are going to hold a party.

IN CLASS

Play the games, sing the songs, eat the food, and have a great party. Remind the children to offer food to their guests in English.

This can be an end of term or end of course party and you can invite other classes. The children can make decorations for the classroom, for example, streamers, paper chains, and place settings.

Project 2
Block of flats

Description of the project

In this project, the students create an imaginary block of flats. Each flat has its own furniture, family, and pets. The people in the flats meet, have parties, and go to school.

Main products of each activity

On completion of the project the class will have achieved/produced the following:

2.1 Rooms in the flat
A room in a block of flats

2.2 Furniture for the flat
Furniture to go in the room

2.3 Family tree
A family tree mobile

2.4 The people who live in the flat
Puppets of the family

2.5 Guess who!
A description and picture of a member of the family

2.6 Pets
A model pet

2.7 Lost!
A 'lost' poster and a cartoon story
A model playground

2.8 Fun club
A board game

2.9 Family scrapbook
A scrapbook containing pictures, writing, photographs, diagrams, and so on, related to the family who live in the flat

2.10 Project display
A display of the children's work from all the activities, for friends and family.

Language and skills

Activity	Grammatical and functional	Vocabulary	Skills
2.1 **Rooms in the flat**	*There is/There are* *How many …?* *What colour …?* *Where do you live?*	Rooms: *wall, window, door, carpet, curtains* Colours Numbers	**Listening:** to and following instructions **Speaking and writing:** asking and answering questions; describing a room orally and in writing **Other:** colouring; cutting; gluing
2.2 **Furniture for the flat**	Prepositions: *near, next to, in front of, behind, on, under* Questions with *to be*	Furniture: *table, chair, sofa, bed* Colours Names of room in a house/flat	**Listening:** to a description **Speaking:** describing a room; asking questions: *Is it near the armchair?* **Writing:** a short description of a room **Other:** cutting; gluing; talking about the room
2.3 **Family tree**	*Have got* Questions: *Have you got (any cousins)? How many brothers have you got?* Possessive adjective: *my*	Family relationships: *grandmother, grand-father, mother (mum), father (dad), sister* Hair/eye colour	**Listening:** to instructions and to each other's presentations **Speaking:** giving a short presentation; asking questions **Writing:** a family tree **Other:** painting; cutting out; tying
2.4 **The people who live in the flat**	Introductions Descriptions	Parts of the body: *eye, nose, mouth, leg, head, hair* Hair/eye colour Clothes	**Listening:** to instructions for the game, song, and puppet-making **Speaking:** singing the song and introducing themselves **Other:** painting; gluing

2.5 **Guess who!**	*Have got* Possessive adjectives: *his, her* Adjectival order: *short, red, hair* Question: *What colour is (her hair)? It's … .* *He is wearing a red sweater and blue shorts* contrasted with *He wears (glasses)*	Describing people: *curly/straight, long/short, red/brown/grey hair* Clothes Colours Numbers up to 100	**Listening:** to descriptions of people **Speaking:** giving a description of clothes in a fashion show **Writing and reading:** a short description **Other:** cutting out; colouring
2.6 **Pets**	Adjectives to describe characteristics Possessive adjectives *his/her* Questions: *What's he like?* *What does he like (doing)?*	Pets: *cat, dog, hamster, rabbit, snake*, and so on Parts of the body: *paw, tail, nose, ears*	**Listening:** to descriptions **Speaking:** talking about a pet **Writing:** a short description **Other:** making a model pet
2.7 **Lost!**	Past simple tense, regular and irregulars Prepositions: *through, down, up, over, under, on, in, out of, into*	House/flat: *door, window, wall, fence, dustbin* Playground or park: *swings, bench, lake, ducks*	**Reading:** a story about a lost pet **Listening** to a story **Speaking:** telling a story. **Writing:** a description of a lost pet, and part of a story **Other:** drawing cartoon pictures; making items for a model playground
2.8 **Fun club**	Asking and answering questions about hobbies: *What's your hobby?* *I collect football posters* Introductions	Hobbies and sports Card and board games	**Listening and speaking:** socializing; playing
2.9 **Family scrapbook**	Revision and extension of all structures in the project	Revision of all vocabulary from previous activities	**Other:** co-operation
2.10 **Project display**	Practice of a range of structures from the project	Practice of vocabulary from the project	**Speaking:** giving a talk to visitors

2.1   Rooms in the flat

LEVEL

Elementary and above

AGE GROUP

8–11

TIME

60 minutes

DESCRIPTION

The children make a room which they will fill with furniture and an imaginary family in later lessons. The rooms will eventually be stacked on top of each other to make a block of flats. The class start a web of house/flat vocabulary.

LANGUAGE

There is/There are; How many …? What colour …? Where do you live? Wall, door, window, living-room, bedroom, bathroom, kitchen; revision of colours and numbers.

SKILLS

Colouring; cutting; gluing.

MATERIALS

A box for each child or group (shoe boxes are ideal), they do not need lids; coloured pens or paints; paper (wallpaper or decorated wrapping paper); cloth material for curtains and/or carpets; glue; scissors; magazines ('Ideal Home' type) with pictures of different rooms; flashcards of: *room, door, window, wall, floor, carpet, curtains,* and *picture,* one set of pictures and one set of words; sticky labels with the words on.

PREPARATION

1 Collect the materials needed.
2 Photocopy the flashcards (pictures and words) of: *room, door, window, wall, floor, carpet, curtains,* and *picture.*
3 Make a room yourself to show as a model.
4 Copy a large version of the spidergram (see photocopiable Worksheet 2.1) on to a large piece of paper, for display on the classroom wall.

IN CLASS

1 Introduce and practise the question: *Where do you live?* And the answer(s): *I live in a house/flat in (Madrid/Hong Kong).* Let the children walk around, asking and answering the question. They can name their suburb or street if they all live in the same city.
2 Using the pictures and flashcards, elicit and practise the names of the rooms in a house or flat: *living-room, kitchen, bathroom, bedroom,* and so on. If necessary, revise colours by asking: *What colour's this room?* Start a class web by filling in the spaces together. The children then copy the words on to their own web (see Worksheet 2.1).
3 Use flashcards to present and practise: *room, door, window, wall, floor, carpet, curtains,* and *picture.* Give out the labels to individual children, and tell them to stick the written words on the cards around the classroom: *window* on the window, *door* on the door, and so on. Add these words to the web.

4 Make the rooms:

    a Divide the children into pairs or groups of three or four. Let the children decide which room they want to make, or see 'Variation', below. It's all right if they all want to make living-rooms or bedrooms, though an entire block of bathrooms would look funny!

    b Give each pair/group a choice of the number and position of windows and doors, colours, paper, cloth, and so on so each room is different. Demonstrate how to cut the wallpaper to fit the inside of the box.

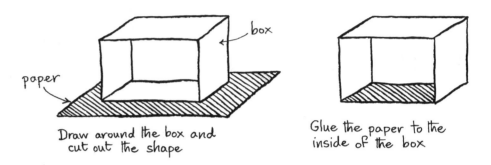

Draw around the box and cut out the shape

Glue the paper to the inside of the box

5 When the rooms are finished, at the end of the lesson or in a later lesson, the children ask and answer questions about them. One pair/group stands at the front holding their room so that the rest of the class can't see it. The teacher and the class ask questions—*What colour's the carpet? What colour are the walls? How many windows are there?* The children answer, and the others guess what room it is. The pair/group then shows the class their room and tell the class the answer.

FOLLOW-UP 1

The children write a description of their room in class, or for homework. They can complete a gap-fill:

My room

You can use some of these words to put in the spaces to describe your room: *is, are, picture, carpet, window, door, curtains, one, two, three, red, yellow, green, blue, white, black, pink.*

In my room there ___ ___ d___, and ___ w_____ . The walls ___ ___,

the c_____ is _____ , and ___ c_____ are _____ . There ___ ___

p_____ on the wall.

FOLLOW-UP 2

See 2.9 'Family scrapbook' for ideas of further activities. Or you can give a written description of your room as a model for the children to follow.

VARIATION

The children could work together in groups or 'families'—each family is responsible for producing all the rooms in a flat, for example, a living-room, a bedroom, a bathroom, and a kitchen.

2.2 Furniture for the flat

LEVEL

Elementary and above

AGE GROUP

8–11

TIME

60 minutes

DESCRIPTION

The children make the furniture to go in the room they have made in the previous activity.

LANGUAGE

Prepositions: *near, next to, in front of, behind, on, under*; furniture; colours; names of rooms in the house/flat; asking questions: *Is it near the armchair?*

SKILLS

Cutting; gluing; talking about your room.

MATERIALS

Pictures of furniture—magazines with photographs and pictures of furniture for the children to cut out; a photocopy of Worksheet 2.2; scissors; coloured pens; glue, and stiff card.

PREPARATION

1 Make some furniture as an example to show the children, put it in the room that you made in 2.1 'Rooms in the flat'.
2 Prepare some furniture flashcards.

IN CLASS

1 Tell the children to look at the class web: rooms in a flat, which they made in the last activity. Ask the children which kind of furniture you find in each room. Use the pictures to help them. Add the vocabulary to the web, for example: *Bedroom: bed, carpet, chair. Living-room: television, sofa, armchair.* Tell the children to copy the words on to their web.
2 Put the children into groups of three or four (as for activity 2.1), then give out the magazines and tell them to find pictures of furniture to put in their rooms. Tell the children to cut out the pictures, stick them on to stiff card, and then trim the pictures carefully.
3 Show the children how to stick a folded piece of card on to the back of the picture, so that it stands up (see diagram).

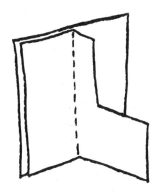 

4 The children arrange the furniture in their room.

5 Get the children to walk around and look at each other's rooms. You can teach them to say *That's nice.*

6 Using some of the furniture and rooms the children have made, demonstrate and practise the prepositions: *near, next to, in front of, behind, on,* and *under.*

7 Put the children in pairs, sitting opposite each other across a table—one child has a room facing towards him or her and the other has a piece of paper and a pencil. The child with the room arranges the furniture and then describes what is in the room and where the furniture is, for example: *the sofa is near the window, the table is next to the sofa, the television is on the table.* The other child tries to draw the room according to the description. They can ask questions, for example: *Is it near the door?* They try to make their picture as accurate as possible.

8 Put the flats together and, with the children, decide on a name for the building, for example: *English Tower.* Give numbers to the different flats so each has an address.

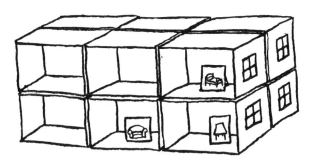

staple the rooms
together, or
stick with tape

9 Store the flats carefully—ideally on tables at the side of the room. They will be used in other activities.

VARIATION 1

Play a game of 'Pairs' to help the children remember the vocabulary:

a Photocopy Worksheet 2.2 on to quite thick paper. You need two sheets for each game.

b Cut out the rectangles and shuffle the two sets of words together to make a pack. You need one pack for each group of four to six children.

c Each group spreads the cards face down on the floor or table.

d Each child has a chance to turn over two cards, without moving them from their position.

e As they turn over each card, they say the word. If the cards are the same, the child keeps the two cards and has another turn. If the cards are different, the cards are turned face down again and it is the next child's turn. The game continues until all the cards have been paired. The 'winner' is the person with the most cards at the end of the game.

VARIATION 2

The children can add to the description of their room from the last lesson. Do an example all together on the board, perhaps using your room.

EXAMPLE

> My room
> In my room there is a door, and two windows.
> The walls are blue, the carpet is green, and the curtains are yellow. There are three pictures on the wall. There's a sofa near the window and an armchair next to the sofa. There is a table and on the table there is a television.

The children's writing can be put in their scrapbooks (see 2.9 'Family scrapbook'), or displayed on the wall.

FOLLOW-UP

See 2.9 'Family scrapbook' for ideas of further activities.

2.3 Family tree

LEVEL

Elementary and above

AGE GROUP

8–11

TIME

60 minutes

DESCRIPTION

The children invent a family to live in their flat. They then make a mobile to illustrate their family tree.

LANGUAGE

Have you got (any cousins)? How many brothers have you got?
possessive adjective: *my*; family members; hair and eye colour.

SKILLS

Painting; cutting out; tying; listening to instructions and to each other's presentations.

MATERIALS

Coloured crayons; felt tip pens or paints; for the mobile: stiff card, cotton thread, two thin wooden sticks per mobile, glue, scissors, and paper.

PREPARATION

1 Make an example mobile to show the children.

2 Collect or draw pictures of a mixture of people. You can ask the children to bring in real photos of members of their family.

3 Make some flashcards with family vocabulary, for example: *grandmother, aunt,* and so on.

IN CLASS

1 Show the children the pictures you have made/collected and stick them on the board. Ask the children who they think the *grandparents* are, who they think the *mother* and *father* might be, and who their *children* are. Arrange some of the pictures on the board like a family tree.

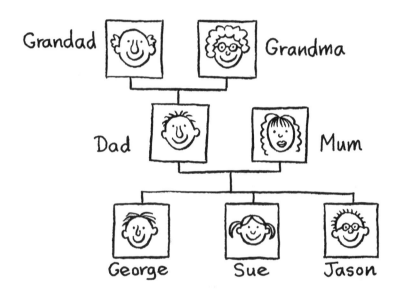

2 Practise the names of different relationships using the flashcards. Stick the names under the pictures on the board. You can teach *uncle, aunt, cousin, niece* or stick to simple family relationships, for example: *mother* and *daughter*, and so on.

3 Practise describing some of the family members together and write sentences on the board next to the photographs of the family, *Aunt Belinda has got black hair and blue eyes. Maria has got blonde hair.*

4 Show the children your mobile and explain that they are going to invent and make their own family of people who live in their flat.

5 Give the people on the mobile names. Play the role of one of the characters and talk about your 'family'. Get the children to ask you questions, *Have you got any cousins? Yes I've got two. George has blonde hair and Adam has red.*

6 Put the children into groups of three or four, as for activity 2.1.
Together, they must decide how many people they want to have
in their family, what their relationships are, what their names are,
and what colour hair and eyes they have.

7 In their groups, the children then make their own mobile.

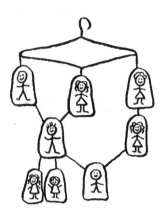

Making the mobile

a Each group draws a family tree and decides who they will have in
the family who lives in their flat (no more than six people).

b Each child in the group chooses which family member(s) they
will draw.

c They draw or paint a picture of the 'person' on a piece of card.
They can make their person as realistic or imaginative as they
wish. You can help them to think carefully about the clothes their
people are wearing by asking them questions as they work: *Is she
wearing a skirt or trousers? What colour is his T-shirt?* and so on.

d When the picture is dry, they cut it out and paint or draw the
back of the person.

e All the pictures should be hung from the mobile. The
grandparents should be at the top of the mobile and the children
at the bottom.

f Hang the mobiles around the room at eye height for the children.
They can be hung on strong cord across the corners of the room.

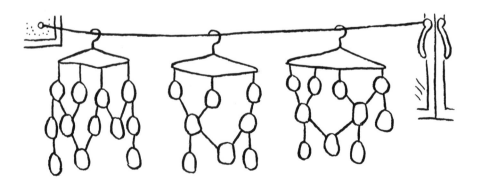

g In turn, each group 'presents' their mobile to the rest of the class. They take the role of one of the 'people' and talk about their 'family'. The other children can prepare questions to ask, for example: *What's your brother's name? Have you got any cousins?*

FOLLOW-UP
The children save the diagram of their family tree to put in their family scrapbook.

See 2.9, 'Family scrapbook' for ideas of further activities.

2.4 The people who live in the flat

LEVEL
Elementary and above

AGE GROUP
8–11

TIME
60 minutes

DESCRIPTION
The children make stick puppet models of their block of flats family (see photocopiable Worksheet 2.4).

LANGUAGE
Parts of the body, for example: *eye, nose,* and *mouth*; hair/eye colour; clothes; describing appearance.

SKILLS
Cutting; painting; gluing; singing songs; listening to instructions.

MATERIALS
Stiff card; coloured pens, pencils, or paints; scissors; coloured wool (for hair); drinking straws, or thin wooden sticks or canes; sticky tape.

PREPARATION
1 Make a stick puppet person to show the children.
2 Photocopy enough templates (Worksheet 2.4) on to card for each group of children to draw around and make their family.

IN CLASS
1 Revise/teach parts of the body. You can do this by:
- drawing a large person on the board, or around a child on a sheet of paper, and then labelling the parts of the body together
- playing 'Simon says':
Simon says touch your nose—everybody must touch their nose. If you say, *touch your nose* without saying *Simon says*, the children mustn't touch their nose, if they do, they are 'out'
- singing 'Head and shoulders, knees and toes', and doing the actions:

Head and shoulders, knees and toes (traditional)

Head   and shoul-ders, knees and   toes,   knees and toes,

Head   and shoul-ders,knees and   toes, knees and toes,   And

eyes,   and   ears,   and   mouth,   and   nose,

Head   and shoul-ders,knees and   toes,   knees and toes.

2 Show your puppet. Help the children, as a class, to talk about his/her appearance and what he/she is wearing, for example: *She's got blonde hair and blue eyes. What's she wearing?*, and so on.

3 Explain that the children are going to make their puppet family.

Making the puppet

a Put the children into groups of three or four. Give the groups of children the template of the family members. Limit the number to 5–6 people for the flat, depending on how many children there are in each group.

b Tell the children to draw around the templates on to stiff card. They then cut out the figures. The children draw faces on the people and colour the bodies. They can make hair out of coloured wool and stick it on to the heads of the people. Explain that the children should try to make the people look like the figures in their family tree with the same coloured hair and eyes, but with different clothes. Encourage them to draw or paint the clothes and shoes in some detail, using different colours, stripes, spots. Go round commenting on the puppets as they work: *Oh, yours has got brown hair and she's wearing a nice green shirt*, and so on.

4 Stick the straws or sticks of wood to the backs of the figures with sticky tape. The children can now use the figures as stick puppets.

5 They can show each other their puppets by going around the room and letting the puppets introduce themselves: *Hello, I'm (Jan). I live at number (5). Hi, my name's (Robert). I live at number (10).*

6 Store them by sticking the straws or sticks into lumps of modelling clay.

| VARIATION | If you are waiting for the paint to dry, you can play 'Simon says' as in step 1. |

| FOLLOW-UP | See 2.9 'Family scrapbook' for ideas of further activities. |

2.5 Guess who!

LEVEL	**Elementary and above**
AGE GROUP	**8–11**
TIME	**60 minutes (extra time for the Follow-up)**
DESCRIPTION	The children choose a member of their 'flat family', describe them and talk about what they are wearing and always wear, then write a description of their person's appearance.
LANGUAGE	*Have got*; possessive adjectives: *his, her*; *What colour is (her hair)? It's … . He is wearing …* contrasted with *He wears …* ; describing people; clothes; colours; numbers up to 100.
SKILLS	Cutting out; colouring.
MATERIALS	Pictures of the 'people' you drew or collected for 2.3 'Family tree'; the stick puppet you made for 2.4 'The people who live in the flat'; photocopies of Worksheet 2.5.
IN CLASS	1 Using the pictures and your puppet, practise language to describe people's appearance. Make the language as complex or as simple as is appropriate for your class.

This is Jane/Peter …

She's got long/short hair.
He's got blue/green/brown eyes.
He's got a big/small nose/a beard/a moustache.

What colour is her hair? It's brown.
What colour are her eyes? Green.

He wears glasses.

What's she wearing today?
She's wearing a green dress and white trainers.

Point out that *wears* is used to describe something that is always true, for example: *glasses*, and *is wearing* for things that change, for example: *a jumper* or *trousers*. You can contrast the same people in the family tree mobile and the puppets if they are wearing different clothes.

2 Play a game to help the children remember the structures and the vocabulary:

a The children all sit on chairs in a circle facing inwards.

b Start the game by saying: *Everyone who's got (long hair) change places*, or *Everyone who's wearing (jeans) change places*, or *Everyone who wears glasses change places*. The children have to get up and sit down again in a different chair. Play for several rounds.

c Say something that applies to you, so that you sit down in one of the chairs. One of the children will be left without a chair. That person gives the next instruction and sits down in the first empty chair as they change seats. Another child is left without a seat and gives the next instruction, and so the game continues.

3 Together, write a description of your puppet on the board.

> This is Fred. Fred is 98. He has long, grey hair and green eyes. He wears glasses. Today, he is wearing a white shirt and black trousers.

4 The children each choose one of the members of their 'flat family' from their block of flats, and write a short description of their person on a separate piece of paper. Go around the classroom helping them.

5 Put all the puppets around the classroom where the children can see them. Collect all the written descriptions and muddle them up. Give a description to each member of the class—make sure you don't give them their own piece of paper. The children walk around the classroom and try to identify the correct puppet from the written description. When they find the correct person, they should put the description next to the puppet.

6 The descriptions (after being corrected) can be stuck into the 'family scrapbook' and the children can draw an accompanying picture of the person for homework.

FOLLOW-UP

The children make some clothes for their puppet people. Photocopy enough clothes templates (see Worksheet 2.5) for each child in the class on to white paper. The children choose one of their puppets to dress and cut out and colour the clothes. They can then have a fashion show when they each parade their person and explain what their 'model' is wearing, for example: *This is Jane, she is wearing a*

lovely green dress and red boots … . At the end of the project the
clothes and a short description can be put in the 'family scrapbook'.
See 2.9, 'Family scrapbook' for ideas of further activities.

2.6 Pets

LEVEL **Elementary and above**

AGE GROUP **8–11**

TIME **60 minutes**

DESCRIPTION The children make pets for their flat family.

LANGUAGE Adjectives to describe characteristics; possessive adjectives: *his* and
her; *What's he like? What does he like (doing)?* pets: *cat, dog, hamster,
rabbit, snake,* and so on; parts of the body: *paw, tail, nose,* and *ears.*

SKILLS Making a model pet.

MATERIALS **Bodies and heads:** cardboard tubes, matchboxes, modelling clay,
small potatoes; **fur:** cotton wool, and wool; **legs:** matchsticks,
toothpicks, cocktails sticks, pipe cleaners; **faces:** buttons, drawing
pins, sequins, small coloured stars, circles; strong glue; pictures of
pets (ask the children to bring in any photos of their own pets).

PREPARATION Collect enough materials for each child to be able to make an
imaginative pet.

IN CLASS
1 Make a list of possible pets on the board. Ask the children who
   have brought photographs of their pets to show the pictures to the
   class, and say something about them. Provide language as it is
   needed, for example: *This is my cat. His name is Sooty. He's black
   and white. He's got a long tail and white paws. He likes playing with
   paper. He's very greedy.*

2 Introduce and practise words to describe the characteristics of
   pets: *funny, friendly, naughty, clever, greedy. She likes playing/
   sleeping/eating/running,* and so on.

3 Make a pet together, practising the language of body parts: *What
   shall we use for the body/head/eyes?* Then, together, bring the pet to
   life: *What's his/her name? What's she like? What does she like doing?*,
   getting suggestions from the class. Put the last three questions
   and some responses on the board.

4 Practise the questions and check that the children understand the
   difference between *What's he like?* and *What does he like?*

5 The children use the materials available to make their own pets
   for their 'flat family'. Encourage them to be as creative as
   possible—it does not have to look like a real animal. Tell them to

give the pet a name, characteristics, and decide what it likes doing.

6 The children take it in turns to show their finished pets to the class. In large classes, divide the children into groups of five or six. The children ask the questions on the board, and the person talking about their pet answers.

7 The pets can now be placed inside the rooms in the block of flats.

FOLLOW-UP

The children write two or three sentences about their pet: its name, some characteristics, and what it likes doing. With lower-level students you can give some of the words and the children fill in the spaces:

My pet

This is my pet. His/her name is _____.

He/she is _____,

and he/she likes _____.

Photocopiable © Oxford University Press

The description can be put in the 'family scrapbook' with a picture of the pet.

See 2.9 'Family scrapbook' for ideas of further activities.

2.7 Lost!

LEVEL

Elementary and above

AGE GROUP

8–11

TIME

60 minutes

DESCRIPTION

The children create a poster, and write a description of their lost pet. They complete a cartoon story about the pet. They make a playground to go next to their block of flats.

LANGUAGE

Simple past tense; prepositions: *through, down, up, over, under, on, in, into, out of*; house/flat: *door, window, wall, fence, dustbin*; playground or park: *swings, bench, lake, ducks*.

SKILLS

Drawing cartoon pictures; making items for a model playground; listening to a story.

MATERIALS

The pets made in activity 2.6 'Pets'; flashcards with the following words: *through, window, down, stairs, out of, door, under, fence, into, playground, on, swings, in, lake, ducks, sandwiches, up, ladder, over wall, into, dustbin*; Worksheet 2.7; stiff card; paper; sticks or wooden pencils; cotton thread; coloured pens or paint; modelling clay; yoghurt pot; scissors; glue; a large piece of cardboard.

PREPARATION

1 Gather the materials needed in individual bags or boxes to make the different parts of the playground.
2 Photocopy Worksheet 2.7—one for each child.
3 Prepare a 'Lost!' poster of your pet.

IN CLASS

1 Pretend to have lost your pet (the one you made in activity 2.6). Look for him/her around the classroom, calling his/her name. You can ask: *Is (Sooty) under your chair? Is he behind the door? Is he in the cupboard?* and so on.
2 Show your 'Lost!' poster.

3 The children make a 'Lost!' poster of their pet. They write their pet's name, description, and address, and draw or paint a picture of their pet.
4 Pretend to 'find' your pet and then tell the children the story of what happened to him, using large copies of the pictures from the worksheet. As you tell the story, put the pictures on the board.

> (Sooty's) adventure
> (Sooty) went through the window, down the stairs, and out of the door. Then he went under the fence and into the playground. He played on the swings, he swam in the lake, he chased the ducks, and he ate some sandwiches. He went up the ladder, and over the wall. Then he fell into the dustbin and he couldn't get out.

5 Use actions with the pictures to demonstrate the prepositions, and repeat the story with the children prompting where necessary. During the third or fourth telling, introduce the flashcards as you use the following words: *through, window, down, stairs, out of, door, under, fence, into, playground, on, swings, in, lake, ducks, sandwiches, up, ladder, over wall, into, dustbin*. Stick the words on the board under the pictures.

6 Give each child a copy of Worksheet 2.7. The children copy the words from the board into the gaps on the worksheet.

7 Tell them to draw their pet in each picture to make a cartoon story.

FOLLOW-UP 1

The children make a playground to go next to their block of flats.

a Divide the class into groups. Each group makes at least one item for the playground. If possible, let them choose what they want to make. There can be several of some items: *trees, ducks, benches, dustbins, flowers,* and *swings*.

b As you put the items together on the card next to the flats, make sure all the children know what the items are called.

c You can use the model playground and one of the model pets to act out the story again.

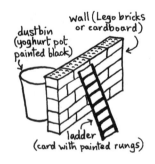

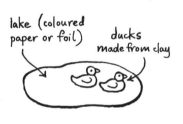

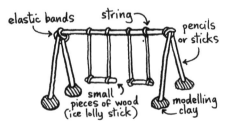

See 2.9 'Family scrapbook' for ideas of further activities.

2.8 Fun club

LEVEL

Elementary and above

AGE GROUP

8–11

TIME

60 minutes

DESCRIPTION

It is common for a block of flats to have a social area where the people who live in the flats meet to play games and socialize. The children make a 'fun club' where the people get together to talk about their hobbies and play games such as 'Bingo' and 'Snap'.

LANGUAGE

Asking and answering questions about hobbies.

SKILLS

Socializing; playing games.

MATERIALS

A selection of simple card and board games such as 'Snap', and the 'Pairs' game described in activity 2.2; card or stiff paper for making 'Bingo' cards; this can be the traditional game played with numbers or with words of a vocabulary area the children are familiar with, for example: parts of the body, or clothes; pictures illustrating different hobbies and sports. You can ask the children to bring in a picture of any sports or activities they like to practise or watch.

PREPARATION

1 Prepare the room by arranging the furniture and making a sign for the door and for the board: '(Name of the block of flats) fun club'.
2 Before this role play, in a previous lesson, practise playing any of the games you are going to play in the 'fun club'.

IN CLASS

1 Explain (in their own language if necessary) that they are in the '(Name of the block of flats) fun club' where they are going to talk to the other people who live in the flats about their hobbies, and play some games with them.
2 Using the pictures you and the children have brought in, build up a list of hobbies and sports on the board.
3 Practise the vocabulary by playing a miming game: the children take it in turns to mime a hobby or sport from the list and the others have to guess what it is.
4 Practise the questions: *What is/are your (favourite) hobby/hobbies?* And the replies: *I play tennis, I like watching television*, and so on.
5 The children practise asking and answering in pairs. Then do a mingling activity where they have to find at least five other children with different hobbies and write their names down. You can then get some of the children to report back to the class: *Marie's hobby is horse riding, James likes watching football, Ellie likes swimming, Rachel plays computer games, and my hobby is listening to music.*
6 Tell the children to pretend it is the weekend and they are meeting their friends from the block of flats at the 'fun club' to talk and play. They each choose to be one of the people from their flat family (probably one of the children). They can decide what hobbies their person has (they can be different from their own). If they wish, they can hold the puppet of the person they are playing and talk through it.

7 They are meeting some people for the first time so they can start by introducing themselves before they go on to talk about their hobbies: *Hi, I'm (Jim). I live at number (9).*

8 After they have spent some time 'socializing', they can play the games you have prepared in pairs or small groups. Finish with a game of 'Bingo' that everyone participates in. You can give a small prize to the winner.

VARIATION

The people who live in the flats can have a fun club party. They can bring in and/or make some food and add the language of requesting, offering, and accepting, in addition to the socializing language. See 1.11 'More party food', for ideas.

FOLLOW-UP 1

A role play in which the children pretend to be the children from the flats going to school on the school bus. They can talk about their school day and which school subjects and teachers they like and don't like. Some of the children can be new neighbours, going to the school for the first time. Together, create a typical timetable of lessons for them to talk about. If possible, place the chairs in the classroom in rows to simulate a bus. The children can pretend to get on the bus with their school bags. You can be the bus driver or the person who checks the tickets (and their English).

See 2.9 'Family scrapbook' for ideas of further activities.

2.9 Family scrapbook

LEVEL

Elementary and above

AGE GROUP

8–11

TIME

As appropriate for your students

AIMS

Revision and extension of all language covered in the project.

DESCRIPTION

The children each make a scrapbook about their family and the block of flats where the family lives.

LANGUAGE

Revision and extension of all language covered in the project.

SKILLS

Co-operation on a group product.

MATERIALS

Thick paper; coloured crayons; pencils; felt tip pens; paper; glue; scissors, and so on. The individual pages can then be made into a book or pasted into a large ready-bought scrapbook.

PREPARATION

Decide which of the suggestions you would like to use for the scrapbook and have the necessary materials ready.

IN CLASS

The scrapbook ideas can be done as part of the activities that make up this project, or separately, to make the project longer. Some of the activities can be completed as homework.

2.1 Rooms in the flat
- a description of the children's room with accompanying drawing
- the web: *houses and flats*

2.2 Furniture for the flat
- a description of the children's room with accompanying drawing, to include furniture
- the web: *houses and flats*, completed with furniture words
- a photograph of the flat, you can take a photo of each flat and some of all the flats put together so each child has two photos to put in his/her scrapbook
- a letter to a friend describing the children's new flat

2.3 Family tree
- diagram of the family tree
- the children's own real family tree

2.4 The people who live in the flat
- family 'photographs' or portraits of the family members—individually or in groups
- grandma/grandad—life when they were children
- a day in the life of a member of the family

2.5 Guess who!
- descriptions of the family members
- clothes for the puppets
- letters to members of the family telling them about recent news—a new baby

2.6 Pets
- letter describing a new family pet—with photograph/picture
- a visit to the vet

2.7 Lost!
- Lost! poster
- cartoon story of the pet's adventure
- stories and pictures about adventures of members of the family
- a description of a picnic in the playground

2.8 Fun club
- diagram and instructions for a board game that the children design and make, for example, if you land on a certain square you have to answer a question in English or do a forfeit as in 1.7 'Party crackers'
- recipes or menus for the block of flats party
- birthday cards and party invitations to other families in the block of flats
- a school timetable
- a description of a typical/my worst/my best day at school
- the day the roof leaked/the basement flooded/the kitchen caught fire
- postcards home from family members away on holiday and holiday photos

The children in your class will probably have lots of ideas.

2.10   Project display

LEVEL	**Elementary and above**
AGE GROUP	8–11
TIME	**As appropriate for your students**
DESCRIPTION	The children use all the language from the rest of the project to display their work to friends and family.
MATERIALS	The block of flats, furniture, puppet family, and pets; the family scrapbooks; any other things made by the children, related to the project.

PREPARATION

1 With the children, make and send out invitations to the project display.

2 Prepare and practise the questionnaires, presentations, songs, and so on.

3 Assemble the block of flats, and number them so each flat has an 'address'. Put up pictures, writing, posters, and so on, on the classroom wall. Display the 'family scrapbooks'.

4 Display the mobiles.

5 Arrange the furniture. Prepare, and put up 'Welcome' posters.

IN CLASS

The children show their work to their visitors. This can be done in a variety of ways:

a In their groups, the children prepare a quiz about their family with questions which their visitors have to answer, for example:

How many people live in flat number 8?
What is the name of Sarah's sister?
What colour is Grandma's hair?
What happened to Sooty when he got lost?
What did they eat at the party?

The visitors have to look at the flat, the family, and the scrapbook to find the answers.

b Each child prepares a short talk about their flat and family, in English. They each present their talk to their own visitors, while showing them their scrapbook, their puppets, and so on.

c The class prepares a series of presentations which are given to all the visitors together. Each child presents one aspect of the project—one talks about the furniture, one about the family tree mobiles, and so on.

d The whole class presents some of the activities they have done during the project. For example, they can play 'Simon says' and sing the song 'Head and shoulders, knees and toes' from activity 2.4, and play the descriptions game in activity 2.5. Some of the visitors could join in.

e The visitors can be offered refreshments by the children, in English: *Would you like some tea/juice/a biscuit?*

Project 3
Picture story

Description of the project

In this project the children create a number of picture stories. Activities 3.1 to 3.4 are suitable for learners who are lower-intermediate and above. These activities consist of self-contained tasks. Some or all of these activities can also be used to prepare learners who are intermediate and above for the project described in activities 3.5 to 3.10. In this project the children plan, prepare, and make a complete photo story.

Main products of each activity

On completion of the project the class will have achieved/produced the following:

3.1 **Jumbled cartoons**
A strip-cartoon story

3.2 **Tell me a story**
An original story based around a photograph

3.3 **Guess the story**
A story adapted from a traditional song

3.4 **Story lucky dip**
An original story based on a random selection of pictures

3.5 **Story types**
A recreation of a well-known story

3.6 **Creating a story**
An original story plan

3.7 **Behind the scenes**
A plan that will be used for 'shooting' their story – scenes, costumes, and props

3.8 **Making the storyboard**
A storyboard—action and dialogue

3.9 **Taking pictures**
Photographs that tell the story

3.10 **Creating a photo story**
Photo story—pictures, dialogue, and text

Language and skills

Activity	Grammatical and functional	Vocabulary	Skills
3.1 Jumbled cartoons	Dialogues past simple	Depends on the cartoon strip used	**Speaking:** making suggestions **Writing:** dialogue in speech bubbles; cartoon captions
3.2 Tell me a story	Present simple and present continuous to describe pictures Past simple for narrative	Family photographs holidays pets	**Speaking and listening:** describing photographs **Writing:** a short story **Other:** gluing
3.3 Guess the story	Past simple Future with *will*	Animals and insects in the song: *fly, spider, cat, dog*	**Listening:** to a song/story **Speaking:** singing the song/ telling the story **Writing:** copying the words of the song; writing their own story **Other:** drawing
3.4 Story lucky dip	Past simple and past continuous for narrative Linking words	Various—depends on the photographs you select	**Listening and speaking:** group discussion when inventing their stories **Writing:** captions for their picture stories **Other:** gluing
3.5 Story types	Past simple Past continuous Adverbs and conjunctions: *while, then, finally, next*	Story genres: *horror, science fiction, fairy tale, romance*	**Listening:** to the teacher telling a story **Speaking:** telling a story **Reading:** a story
3.6 Creating a story	Past simple Past continuous with *while* Adverbs and conjunctions: *suddenly, then, finally, next*	Vocabulary as needed for writing the individual stories	**Writing:** making notes; a short story **Reading:** editing each other's work
3.7 Behind the scenes	No specific grammar points	Appearance of people and scenes	**Listening:** to one another. **Speaking:** discussing and making decisions; describing **Writing:** lists **Other:** drawing, painting

3.8 **Making the** **storyboard**	Present simple Present continuous Past continuous with *while*	Vocabulary as needed for the individual stories	**Writing:** sentences for the story-board; dialogue; notes; lists **Speaking:** discussing and making decisions **Other:** drawing, gluing
3.9 **Taking pictures**	Instructions and requests	Jobs and responsibilities in the film industry: *director, producer,* *camera person, special* *effects*	**Speaking:** giving instructions and making requests **Writing:** labels **Other:** taking photographs
3.10 **Creating a photo** **story**	Practice of grammar from other activities	Vocabulary as needed for the individual stories	**Speaking:** discussing and deciding **Writing:** dialogue and narrative text of a story **Reading:** editing texts **Other:** cutting out, gluing

3.1 Jumbled cartoons

LEVEL	**Lower-intermediate and above**
AGE GROUP	**8–13**
TIME	**30 minutes**
DESCRIPTION	Each group has a short cartoon strip where the pictures have been cut up and jumbled, and the words in speech bubbles have been removed. The children put the pictures in the right order, and decide which words to write in the speech bubbles. They also write captions underneath each picture.
LANGUAGE	Dialogue; past simple.
SKILLS	Working as a group.
MATERIALS	A set of the photocopied and jumbled cartoon strip for each group or pair of children (about four pictures would be ideal), see the example.
PREPARATION	1 Find a suitable cartoon strip. A strip from a children's comic or a newspaper would be fine, as long as the story is obvious from looking at the pictures. It doesn't matter if the cartoon is not in English, as you are going to blank out the words in the speech bubbles. You could use the cartoon strip below:

Photocopiable © Oxford University Press

2 Blank out the words in the dialogue.

3 Photocopy the cartoon strip and cut it up. It's a good idea to enlarge it before copying, to allow the children enough room to write in the speech bubbles.

IN CLASS

1 Give each pair or group of children the four cut-up pictures from each strip, and ask them to decide what order the pictures should go in. Check the answers and make sure that everyone agrees.

2 Ask the children for suitable words or phrases to put in the first speech bubble. Write the possible answers on the board.

3 Ask each pair or group to think of words for the remaining bubbles. Tell the children that a few words will be enough. The children write the words in the speech bubbles.

4 Give each pair or group a sheet of paper to stick their cartoon pictures on. Display the cartoon strips on the wall, or pass them around the class for the children to see each other's work.

FOLLOW-UP

To give the children practice in using the past simple and in writing skills, you can ask them to tell the story by writing a caption for each picture. They could do it for homework. There are examples for the 'Fred' cartoon here:

1 Mr Smith's newspaper arrived.

2 He asked his dog Fred to go and fetch it. Fred was feeling sleepy and said 'No'.

3 Mr Smith went to get the newspaper himself.

4 Fred jumped into Mr Smith's chair and went to sleep. Mr Smith was angry.

3.2 Tell me a story

LEVEL

Lower-intermediate and above

AGE GROUP

8–13

TIME

45 minutes

DESCRIPTION

Each child creates a story around a photograph they bring to the lesson. They stick the photograph on to a piece of paper and write the story underneath.

LANGUAGE

Present simple and present continuous for description; past simple for telling a story in the past; vocabulary of families.

SKILLS

Telling stories inspired by family photographs; gluing.

MATERIALS

Photographs brought in by the children; extra photographs in case a child forgets, or doesn't have one; glue; paper; card.

PREPARATION

Ask each child to bring a favourite photograph into school. The photograph can have anything as its subject, but encourage the children to bring in photos of family members, pets, or holidays.

IN CLASS

1 Show the children your own photograph and explain what is in the picture, for example: *This is my cat, Sooty. He's in the dining-room on the table.*

2 Help the children with vocabulary to describe their photo. Ask the children to describe their own photograph to the person next to them. They can describe the photo, then show it.

3 Ask the class to look at your photograph again and help you invent a short story about what they can see.

One day Sooty was alone in the house. He saw some chicken on the table in the dining-room. He jumped on the table and ate the chicken. When I came home I was angry. But my husband said: 'It's your fault, not Sooty's. You left the chicken on the table!'

4 Tell the children to write a story about their photograph. They can start their story: *One day … .* All the stories will be different, so you need to help the children with their vocabulary. Make sure they tell the story in past time.

5 When you have checked the stories, ask the children to stick their photographs into their books or on to a piece of card, and write their stories underneath.

6 Display the stories for the whole class to see. Give them time to read each other's stories.

VARIATION 1

Step 4 can be completed for homework and you can check it before they write a final copy under the photograph.

VARIATION 2

The activity can be done in pairs or groups. The children have to find a way of using both/all of their photographs in one story.

3.3 Guess the story

LEVEL

Lower-intermediate and above

AGE GROUP

8–13

TIME

60 minutes

DESCRIPTION

Each child is given a different animal to draw from the story of 'The Old Woman who Swallowed a Fly'. The children draw their pictures and then try to work out the story collectively by looking at all their pictures. The class then change the characters to create their own story.

LANGUAGE

Past simple for narrative; the future using *will*; animals and insects in the song: *fly, spider, bird, cat, dog, cow, horse*; *to swallow*.

SKILLS

Listening to and singing a song; drawing.

MATERIALS

The text of the story of 'The Old Woman who Swallowed a Fly'; if possible, a book of the story to show the children, or pictures.

PREPARATION

1 Write out the names of all the animals in the story on separate pieces of paper.

IN CLASS

1 Give out the pieces of paper with animal names on them. Ask the children to draw whatever is written on their pieces of paper. If there are more children than animals, divide the class into groups and give each child in the group a different animal to draw.

2 When the children have finished drawing, lay all the pictures out on the floor in the middle of the room, or stick them on the wall in the order they come in the song. Ask the children if they know the song or story. Show them a picture of an old woman and sing the song (or tell the story), with appropriate actions.

I know an old woman who swallowed a fly (traditional)

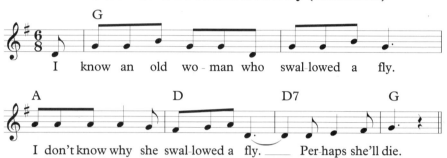

I know an old wo-man who swal-lowed a fly.
I don't know why she swal-lowed a fly. ___ Per-haps she'll die.

3 See if they can guess what comes next. If they can't, help them.

I know an old wo-man who swal-lowed a spi-der, that
wrig-gled and jig-gled and tick-led in-side her, She
swal-lowed the spi-der to catch the fly. I don't know why she
swal-lowed a fly. ___ Per-haps she'll die.

and so on, each time substituting the lines below.

(*a bird*) *How absurd, to swallow a bird*
(*a cat*) *Fancy that, to swallow a cat*
(*a dog*) *What a hog, to swallow a dog*
(*a cow*) *I don't know how she swallowed a cow*
(*a horse*) *She's dead, of course.*

4 Practise singing or saying the story a few times. You can give out the children's pictures and get the children to hold them up every time they hear their animal mentioned.

FOLLOW-UP 1

The children can copy the words of the song into their notebooks, and illustrate the song with their own pictures. Some of this can be done for homework.

FOLLOW-UP 2

The class invents its own story along similar lines by changing the main character, the situation, and the animals. It doesn't have to rhyme.

I know an (old man) who (bought a worm)
He bought the worm to catch a fish
He bought the fish to catch a cat.

This can be done together as a class, or in pairs, or groups.

3.4   Story lucky dip

LEVEL

Lower-intermediate and above

AGE GROUP

8–13

TIME

60 minutes

DESCRIPTION

The children pick some random pictures and use them to invent a story. They stick the photographs on a large piece of paper, and write the story captions underneath.

LANGUAGE

Past simple and continuous for narrative; linking words.

SKILLS

Group discussion and story invention; gluing.

MATERIALS

Enough pictures (they could be from magazines) for each group of children to have at least four, for example, two different people or animals, a location, and an object. It would help if the photographs were unusual or exotic enough to help the children's imaginations; large pieces of paper to stick the picture stories on.

PREPARATION

1 Bring in a selection of pictures of people, places, and any interesting objects.
2 Divide the pictures into separate piles: animals or people, places, and objects.
3 Put each pile into a separate bag, so the children have to put their hands inside to take a picture out.

IN CLASS

1 Divide the children into groups of two or three. Each group of children takes it in turns to take a picture out of each bag. Make sure they know the vocabulary for each object, place, or animal, for example, *computer*, *beach*, and *crocodile*.

2 Take your own four pictures out of the bags, and with the whole class, invent a story about them. For example:

One day a crocodile was sleeping on a beach when he saw a boat. In the boat there was a computer. The crocodile thought that the computer was an animal and so he ate it. It made him feel ill but now he's very good at maths!

3 Give the children time to discuss their own pictures in their groups and to create a story using them. Go around the groups helping with vocabulary. At this stage the story can be created orally.

4 Give each group a large piece of paper to stick the photographs on.

5 Tell the children to write the picture story captions underneath each picture and display them for the other groups to see.

VARIATION

Step 5: the written story can be prepared individually for homework. In the next lesson, the children then compare their versions in their groups, decide on any corrections, and write their joint version under the photographs.

3.5 Story types

LEVEL

Intermediate and above

AGE GROUP

11–13

TIME

60 minutes (90 minutes if all grammar activities used)

DESCRIPTION

The children are introduced to the idea of a picture story. This stage is not necessary if you have done some of the preparation activities 3.1–3.4. They look at different types of stories, how a story is structured, and how language is used to express time in a story. 'Little Red Riding Hood' is used as an example here, but you can choose other well-known or popular stories for this activity.

LANGUAGE

Past simple and past continuous to show two actions happening at the same time; adverbs and conjunctions: *while, suddenly, then, finally, next*; types of stories, for example, *horror* and *science fiction*.

SKILLS

Telling a story.

MATERIALS

Examples of picture stories: these can sometimes be found in coursebooks or teenage magazines. A picture story is like a strip cartoon with the story told mainly in pictures or photographs with speech bubbles and some text telling the story underneath each picture.

PREPARATION

1 Find some example picture stories to show the children.

2 Photocopy 'Little Red Riding Hood' (see opposite page) and cut it into strips, one set for each pair of children.

IN CLASS

1 Explain to the class that they are going to make their own picture story in small groups. Show them some examples. Explain that first you are going to look at the structure of a story, using a story everyone knows as an example.

2 Ask the class to list the types of stories that they like and write these on the board, for example, *fairy tales, horror, science fiction, romance, murder,* and *mystery*. Ask the children for examples of each of these types of stories, for example, 'Little Red Riding Hood', 'Dracula', 'The X-Files', and 'Romeo and Juliet'. Ask them why they like these types of stories and write up some of the words beside each type of story.

3 Take one of the stories that everybody in the class knows— perhaps 'Little Red Riding Hood'—and ask the following questions, writing them and the answers on the board.

What kind of story is it?	It's a fairy tale.
When does the story take place?	A long time ago./Many years ago.
Where does the story take place?	In a big forest./In a cottage in the forest.
Who is in the story?	A young girl, her mother, her grandmother, a wolf and a woodcutter.
What are the names of the characters in the story?	Little Red Riding Hood, Mother, Grandmother, The Big Bad Wolf and The Woodcutter.

4 Ask the children to tell you what happens in the story. Don't worry about correcting their language too much at this stage, you want them to tell you the story and what happens in the right order. Repeat their sentences using the correct tenses and structures.

5 Teach/revise the meaning, pronunciation, and past simple of the verbs used in the story that may be unfamiliar: *ask, live, walk, creep, eat, put, arrive, look, reply, say, jump, kill, save, cut.* Write the verbs and their past tense forms on the board.

6 Put the children into pairs, and give them strips of paper with the separate events of the 'Little Red Riding Hood' story on each strip.

<u>One day</u> Little Red Riding Hood's mother asked her to take some apples to her grandmother who lived far away in the forest.

<u>It was a lovely day as</u> Little Red Riding Hood walked through the forest to her grandmother's house.

<u>Meanwhile</u> the big bad wolf was hungry. He crept quietly into grandmother's house and ate her up in one big bite.

<u>Then</u> the big bad wolf put on grandmother's clothes. <u>A little later</u> Little Red Riding Hood arrived at her grandmother's house.

She thought her grandmother looked different: 'What great big eyes you have Grandmother,' she said.

'All the better to see you with my dear,' the wolf replied.

'What great big ears you have Grandmother,' she said.

'All the better to hear you with,' the wolf replied.

'What great big teeth you have Grandmother,' she said.

'All the better to eat you with,' the wolf replied and jumped towards Little Red Riding Hood.

<u>Suddenly</u> the woodcutter arrived and killed the big bad wolf.

Little Red Riding Hood was saved!

<u>Finally</u> the woodcutter cut open the wolf's tummy and grandmother jumped out alive!

7 Ask the children to put the story in the correct order. You can make this activity more difficult by blanking out the verbs and asking them to fill them in from the list you have just revised together on the board.

8 The linking words and phrases, for example: *meanwhile, a little later, suddenly*, can be introduced/taught at this stage, or you could give the children a list of these words/phrases and ask them to insert them into appropriate blanks you make in the story.

9 Ask the children how many 'events' there are in the story and perhaps write them on the board.

Beginning:
Little Red Riding Hood walks through the forest.
The wolf eats the grandmother.
Middle:
Little Red Riding Hood talks to the wolf.
The wolf tries to eat Little Red Riding Hood.
End:
The woodcutter saves Little Red Riding Hood.
The grandmother is saved too.

10 Explain to the children that a good story often has a structure like this and when they make up their stories in the next lesson they will need to keep them quite simple with just a few exciting events.

FOLLOW-UP

Ask the children how the 'Little Red Riding Hood' story might be different if it was set today rather than many years ago. For example: Little Red Riding Hood might have a different name, she might ride a motorbike and live in a big city, she might go to visit her grandmother by train, and so on.

If the children have been taught the second conditional you can use the story to practise:

If Little Red Riding Hood was alive today she would wear a black leather jacket instead of her red cloak. She would ride a big red motorbike.
If Little Red Riding Hood was alive today she would live in a big city and not a large forest.
If Little Red Riding Hood lived in the city she would visit her grandmother every day. She would go by bus.

VARIATION

If the children have been taught the past continuous, you can use the story to practise the concept of two actions happening at the same time. You and the children can then build up the story to incorporate more imagined details.

a Ask the children the following questions:

What was the wolf doing while Little Red Riding Hood was still at home?
He was sleeping.
What was he doing while she was saying goodbye to her mother?
He was feeling hungry.
What was he doing while she was walking through the forest?
He was creeping towards her grandmother's house.
What was her grandmother doing while the wolf was creeping towards her house?
She was baking a cake.

b Write some sample sentences on the board. Expand the sentences using *while* to connect two sentences, using the past continuous, to make one sentence.

While Little Red Riding Hood was walking through the forest, the wolf was creeping towards her grandmother's cottage.
While grandmother was baking a cake, the wolf was creeping in through the door.

c Ask the children to make up some more sentences using *while*; these can be written up on the board or in their books.

3.6 Creating a story

LEVEL	**Intermediate and above**
AGE GROUP	**11–13**
TIME	**90 minutes (or two lessons of 45 minutes, one lesson for planning and one lesson for expanding the notes and writing the story)**
DESCRIPTION	The children create a story in groups of six that they will develop into their photo story.
LANGUAGE	Revision of grammar covered in activity 3.5.
SKILLS	Reading and editing each other's work.
MATERIALS	Examples of picture stories from activity 3.5; large sheets of paper; coloured pencils, or felt tip pens.
PREPARATION	Make a story plan on a large piece of paper to show the children as an example (see step 7 for a suggested story).

IN CLASS

1 Explain to the children that they are going to create the story for their photo story. Remind the children about the stages of a story (3.5).

2 Put the children in groups of six and give them a large piece of paper. Write up the following questions on the board.

Questions	Example answers
What kind of story is it?	fairy tale, romance, horror, science fiction, mystery
When does the story take place?	a long time ago, in 2003, last month
Where does the story take place?	forest, castle, another planet, laboratory, school.
Who is in the story?	a mad scientist, a witch, a monster, a beautiful princess, a magic frog.
What are the names of the characters in the story?	Wilfred the Witch, Princess Penelope, Croak the Frog, Professor Dabble.

3 Ask the children for some example answers, and put these answers on the board (see above) to start them off.

4 The children work together, in their groups, to decide on the components for their story by answering the questions above. They write their answers on their piece of paper with coloured pens. You will have to assist each group with appropriate vocabulary.

5 Encourage the children to add further details to their story plan by asking the groups or the class further questions, for example:

What is the forest like? It's big and dark.
What is the castle like? It's on a hill in the centre of the forest, it's old
and very large and frightening. What does the mad scientist look like?
He has white hair and a big white beard.

6 Give each group another large piece of paper. Explain that the groups must now decide what happens in their story. Show them the example you have made on your sheet of paper.

7 Explain that you don't want them to write lots of details at this point, but to decide on what is going to happen, and in what order. There is an example below.

Our story

1st – A scientist built a space rocket in his laboratory.
2nd – He flew to Mars.
3rd – Some aliens saw the rocket land. They hid and watched the scientist.
4th – The scientist collected some plants and rocks.
5th – The aliens went to say hello to the scientist.
6th – The scientist and the aliens made friends.
7th – The scientist visited the aliens' home, had tea and met the family.
8th – The scientist returned to earth in his rocket. He promised to tell no one about the aliens.
9th – Back on earth the scientist kept in touch with the aliens by e-mail.
10th – The aliens plan to come to visit earth... but that's another story!

---

8 When the children's story plans are complete, explain that they must work in pairs and divide the different parts of the story up. Pair one takes the first three points, pair two, the second three points, and so on. Each pair of children must now expand their part of the story in written form. Encourage the children to use some of the language they practised in activity 3.5: *while* plus past continuous, linkers—adverbs and conjunctions. You will need to assist with appropriate vocabulary and check verb forms. Set a time limit of ten minutes or so.

9 When the pairs have finished expanding their part of the story, the group should read the whole story through together in order. They may want to correct parts of the story or add extra points or details.

10 The story should then be written up neatly. This can be done for homework after you have corrected any mistakes. Each child in the group should have a neat copy of the story to put into their notebooks.

3.7   Behind the scenes

LEVEL	**Intermediate and above**
AGE GROUP	**11–13**
TIME	**60 minutes (longer if you include the painting of the various pictures planned)**

DESCRIPTION

The children work together in their groups to decide on the background scenes and characters for their photo story, where the photographs will be taken, and the costumes and props required.

LANGUAGE

Any grammar and vocabulary used will arise from the children's discussions in groups; there is no explicit language input in this activity.

SKILLS

Discussing and making decisions; describing; drawing and painting.

MATERIALS

Large sheets of paper; coloured pens, pencils, and crayons; highlighter pens; glue; scissors; sheets of white A4 paper; a large cardboard box for each group; examples of picture story planning sketches for each group (see Worksheets 3.7a and b).

PREPARATION

1 Make enough copies of each group's story for every child in the group to have one.

2 Photocopy the examples of picture story planning sketches given here or make your own, following your own storyline, to show the children.

IN CLASS

1 Explain that the children are movie producers. They are now going to plan the background scenes, locations, and the characters and their costumes for their picture story.

2 Give out the photocopied stories to each group. Ask the children to work together in their group. Tell them to read through their own story and underline all the locations in their story with a coloured pen. They must use the same coloured pen for all the locations, for example: *a laboratory* and *on Mars*.

3 When the children have highlighted the locations, they make a list of them on a large sheet of paper in the order that they appear in the story. In the example these would be:

in the scientist's laboratory
flying through space
in the aliens' living-room
in the scientist's office.

4 The children now do the same with the various characters that appear in the story, highlighting them with a different coloured pen as they appear, and listing them on another large sheet of paper.

a scientist
two aliens
the aliens' family.

5 The children must now decide what the characters and locations will look like, and how they are going to show them in their photo story.

Locations

They might decide that they need to paint a picture for some of the scenes, which can then be photographed, or they may be able to adapt an area of the classroom or school. Show them your examples (or use Worksheet 3.7a).

> Locations:
> The scientist's laboratory-photograph in the corner of the classroom by the window.

Characters

For their characters they should decide which of their group will play each character and what they will need to wear. They should make notes together on their sheets of paper. Show them the examples you have prepared for your story to help them (or use the examples on Worksheet 3.7b).

> Characters:
> A scientist- a photograph of Julia, wearing a wig, a white beard, glasses.

6 On a sheet of paper they should draw a sketch of how they would like the location or character to look. Show them your examples. These should not be detailed pictures, just quick sketches.

7 When the children have finished these sketches they stick them on the original large sheets of paper where they made their notes on the locations and characters.

8 The children now decide which props they will need for the characters and locations. They should write this under each picture, for example: *Scientist—wig, white beard made of cotton wool, glasses, white coat.*

9 The children agree who will find and bring in the various items needed. Provide each group with a cardboard box so that they can start collecting their props in a 'prop box' before the next photo story lesson. Display the planning posters on the classroom wall.

10 The children can paint any pictures they have planned in this, or another lesson.

3.8 Making the storyboard

LEVEL	**Intermediate and above**
AGE GROUP	**11–13**
TIME	**60–90 minutes (longer if the children are going to make their props and/or design their costumes in this lesson)**

DESCRIPTION

The children plan and make a detailed storyboard for their photo story. They write a description of what is happening in each scene of their story, and plan any dialogue or thought bubbles required in the final photographs.

LANGUAGE

Revision of all the structures covered in the other parts of the project.

SKILLS

Discussing and making decisions; drawing and gluing.

MATERIALS

Large sheets of paper; A4 sheets of white paper; coloured pens and pencils; scissors; glue, copies of the children's stories; posters; the 'prop box' from 3.7 'Behind the scenes'; a photocopied example of a storyboard, one for each group (see Worksheet 3.8).

PREPARATION

Copy the example of the storyboard given here, or prepare your own using your own story.

IN CLASS

1 Explain that the children are now going to prepare the storyboard for their photo story. A storyboard is a list of pictures and notes which shows the director of the film or photo story which photos he/she needs to take for each scene, in what order the photos need to be arranged, what the characters do in each scene, and what they say. Show the children your example.

2 The children now need to decide how many photographs they are going to have in their story and make their own storyboard. Each photo is like a 'scene' in the story. In their groups, they number the main 'scenes', which they want to turn into photos, in coloured pen on the photocopies of their stories (there shouldn't be more than fifteen photos in the story, ten to twelve is probably enough).

3 The children now write a sentence for each 'scene', which will be turned into a photo, at the bottom of a piece of paper, one piece of paper for each scene. The children should use the present continuous to describe what is happening in each scene.

The scientist is building his rocket in his laboratory.
The rocket is flying through space towards Mars.
The rocket is landing on Mars.

4 Tell the children to draw sketches of each scene on the pieces of paper, above the sentence that they have written. Each child in the group should be responsible for one or two scenes. They

should add any speech bubbles to show the dialogue that will be added to the photographs later (see example).

5 When all the sketches have been finished, and the dialogue has been planned and added to the storyboard, the children stick their pieces of paper or 'scenes' on to a large piece of poster paper in the correct order to make the storyboard.

6 Under each scene, the children add any important notes that they will need to remember when they take the photographs. They add a note saying where the photographs will be taken, referring to their planning poster, 3.7 'Behind the scenes', for example: *photograph in playground, stick on thought bubble, photograph of alien family painting, stick on dialogue bubbles* (see example).

7 The children make a list of any extra props they need to bring in and add to their prop box, for example: *green rubber gloves for alien hands*.

8 Any extra paintings or pictures that are needed for the scenes can be painted and any props made, for example: cotton wool beard.

Here are some other activities in this book which might help when the children are making props and costumes:

Mask making
1.3 'Party masks'

Making costumes
4.4 'Design an outfit for a pop star'

Making model animals
2.6 'Pets'

Inventing fantasy creatures
5.3 'Fantasy creatures'

3.9   Taking pictures

LEVEL	**Intermediate and above**
AGE GROUP	**11–13**
TIME	**60–90 minutes (depending on how many scenes each group needs to set up and photograph)**
DESCRIPTION	The children set up the scenes for their photo stories and take the photographs.
LANGUAGE	Instructions and requests; jobs and responsibilities in the film industry.
SKILLS	Taking photographs.
MATERIALS	One 35mm camera, with automatic focus and flash, per group, (ask the children to bring in their own cameras); one colour film per

group; storyboards from 3.8 'Making the storyboard'; props and paintings from previous activities; white sticky labels; black marker pens.

PREPARATION

1 Plan how you will supervise the different groups as they take their photographs around the school and classroom.

2 Warn the children what they will be doing in this activity so that they come prepared.

IN CLASS

1 Ask the children what special responsibilities people have who make films, for example: in charge of arranging and clearing up the props, in charge of costumes and dressing the characters, in charge of arranging the characters in the scene following the storyboard instructions, in charge of taking the photos, in charge of directing the film, in charge of special effects, and so on. Make a list of these jobs on the board, asking for contributions from the class. Ask the children what the names of the jobs are and provide those they do not know: *camera person, wardrobe, director*, and so on.

2 The children decide who is going to be responsible for the various jobs involved in making their picture story. The children make themselves labels which they wear on their front saying what their jobs are:

Special Effects | Director | Wardrobe | Make up | Camera person | Props

3 You may want to teach/revise the language of instructions and requests at this stage, as the children will be working together and asking or telling each other what to do, for example: *Please could you put the props over there; look up; look more frightened; smile; stand still; Could you help Julia put on her costume, please?* and so on.

4 In their groups, the children decide in what order they are going to take their photographs. The photographs which take place in the same location should be taken at the same time. The children should refer to their storyboards.

5 The children prepare the areas of the classroom that they are going to use for each photograph. One area should be prepared at a time and then tidied up before the next area is prepared, for example: set up the scientist's laboratory in the corner of the classroom first, dress up the child who is going to play the scientist, and place any props in the correct positions. Take the photographs, and then tidy up and move on to the next scene. The children should refer to their storyboards, to ensure they are setting up the scenes in the way they had planned.

6 The children take all their photographs. It is a good idea to take two photographs of each scene, in case one is out of focus or doesn't come out. If the children are taking photographs of any paintings they have made, help them to make sure they get a large enough image and that the picture is in focus. It is best to stick the paintings on the wall when you take photographs of them.

7 Take a photograph of each group when they have finished. Write the name of each group on the film box.

8 Take the films to be developed. You will need them for the next activity.

3.10   Creating the photo story

LEVEL	**Intermediate and above**
AGE GROUP	**11–13**
TIME	**60 minutes**
DESCRIPTION	The children complete their photo stories by putting the photographs they have taken in order, adding dialogue, thought bubbles, and the text which tells the story, under each picture.
LANGUAGE	Revision of the grammar and vocabulary covered in activities 3.5 to 3.9.
SKILLS	Discussion and making decisions; cutting out and gluing.
MATERIALS	Large sheets of coloured paper or stiff card; white sticky labels; coloured pens and pencils; thin black felt tip pens; sticky tape or Blu-Tak; storyboards; developed photographs.
PREPARATION	Develop the photographs that the children took in the last lesson.

IN CLASS

1 Give out the photographs that the children took in the last lesson.

2 The children select the best pictures (they took two pictures of each scene).

3 The children refer to their storyboards and add any dialogue or thought bubbles to the photographs. They cut the right sized dialogue bubbles out of sticky white labels, write the dialogue or thoughts on the bubbles in black felt tip pen, peel off the backing, and stick the bubbles on to the photographs.

4 The children make up any photo montages that they had planned on the storyboard by cutting out and sticking part of one photograph on to another picture, for example: cutting out the face of the scientist and sticking it in the window of the spacecraft.

5 The children then arrange the photographs in the correct order to make their story on the coloured paper or stiff card, leaving a

space for a piece of writing under each photograph. The pictures are then stuck on to the card.

6 Referring to the story each group wrote in 3.6 'Creating a story', the children discuss what they will write under each picture to tell the story. They tell the story again together.

7 Each child in the group chooses two or three pictures, and then writes the accompanying text to go under each picture in draft form.

8 The group reads the pieces of draft writing together and corrects, amends, and edits the texts. You should check the work at this stage for any errors.

9 Each child then writes out his or her part of the story neatly, with corrections, on a piece of white paper which is then stuck underneath the appropriate photograph.

10 Display all the photo stories on the classroom wall.

Reading each other's photo stories. Some ideas for using the photo stories in class.

1 Jumbled stories

a Take two or three photo stories.

b Before the children stick their writing underneath the appropriate pictures (see step 9 above) photocopy the texts.

c Mask the text under the displayed stories by covering it with a piece of card so that the children can't see it.

d Put the children into pairs.

e Make enough copies of each piece of text for every pair of children.

f Muddle up the texts.

g Tell the children to have a look at the photo stories. They should discuss with their partner what they think the story is about as they can't see the writing.

h Sitting together in their pairs, they must sort out the piles of text into two or three separate stories and then put each story in the correct order to match each photograph.

i Unmask the text on the wall and check the answers together.

2 What happened next?

a When the children are putting their photo stories together, save a space for the last picture in the story, but don't stick it on the card.

b Display all the final photos together and write a number under each one.

c Put the children into pairs.

d The children look at all the photo stories and read the text underneath the pictures.

e Together, in pairs, they must decide which is the final picture for each story from the group of final photos.

f Check the answers together and then stick the final photos in the right places on the photo stories.

3 Who did what?

a Ask each group to write three or four questions about their photo story. The answers should be found by reading the text of the story or the thought and speech bubbles, for example: *How did the scientist feel when he saw the aliens approaching?* Answer: *Very scared.*

b Make a list of all the questions. If you want to make it more difficult, muddle up the questions so that they do not follow any particular order.

c Put the children into pairs and ask them to read the stories together, find the answers, and write them down.

d Check the answers together as a class.

4 Running dictation

a Put the children into pairs, child A and child B.

b Write down a list of questions for child A and a list of questions for child B, based on the photo stories.

c Put the photo stories together on one wall or around the room.

d Sit the children together in pairs.

e Child A must ask child B his/her first question, for example, *Where did the scientist live?* Child B must run up to the appropriate photo story, find the answer, run back to child A, and dictate the answer, which child A writes down.

f Child B then asks his/her first question and child A must go and find out the answer.

g Continue until all the questions have been answered.

5 Mini plays

The children can expand their photo stories further by incorporating more dialogue and then acting them out as mini plays.

Project 4
Music

Description of the project

In this project the students explore different aspects of popular music.

Main products of each activity

On completion of the project the class will have produced/achieved the following:

4.1 Design a CD or cassette cover
The design for a cassette or CD cover

4.2 Invent a pop band
A biography of a pop band the students have created
Descriptions of individual members of the band

4.3 A day in the life of a pop star
A cartoon strip telling a day in the life of a pop star

4.4 Design an outfit for a pop star
A poster showing an outfit the students have designed for a pop star

4.5 Fashion show
An outfit which is modelled in a fashion show
A written description to accompany a photograph of the model

4.6 Making music
A musical instrument

4.7 Music from around the world
A postcard from a pop star on tour

4.8 Write a song
The students write/adapt a song

4.9 Mystery band
A completed puzzle

4.10 The ELMAs—The English Language Music Awards
An award ceremony with nominations and acceptance speeches
Awards for different categories

4.11 Make a 'fanzine'
A fanzine—a collection of written and graphic work done throughout the music project

Language and skills

Activity	Grammatical and functional	Vocabulary	Skills
4.1 **Design a CD or cassette cover**	Present simple for description Expressing likes and dislikes: *love, can't stand* Past simple	Types of music: *pop, rock, jazz, classical,* and so on Words and expressions to do with music: *guitar, lead singer, hit record, single, album, tour*	**Speaking:** expressing likes and dislikes and giving opinions **Writing:** the titles of records **Reading:** CD and record covers **Other:** designing and drawing a record cover
4.2 **Invent a pop band**	Present simple to describe characteristics and habits Past simple to talk about specific dates, actions	Clothes Physical appearance	**Speaking:** discussing and creating the history of an imaginary pop band **Writing:** a biography of a pop band **Reading:** written biographies **Other:** cutting and drawing
4.3 **A day in the life of a pop star**	Present simple for describing habitual actions Adverbs of frequency: *usually, always, sometimes, every day*	Words and expressions describing daily routines: *brush my teeth, catch the bus to school, play outside*	**Speaking:** describing daily routines **Writing:** descriptions of their own and other people's routines; captions for a comic strip **Other:** drawing pictures for a comic strip; gluing
4.4 **Design an outfit for a pop star**	Present continuous to describe what someone is wearing	Clothes Adjectives of colour, pattern, size	**Speaking:** deciding on a description **Writing:** captions, short descriptions of clothes **Other:** making a drawing or collage
4.5 **Fashion show**	Present continuous for description	Clothes and accessories	**Speaking:** giving a commentary to a fashion show
4.6 **Making music**	Adverbs and adjectives that describe sound: *It goes … . It makes a … sound*	Vocabulary to describe sounds: *bang, crash, rattle, twang, hiss, splash, tinkle* Musical instruments	**Speaking:** identifying and describing sounds **Writing:** creating words and using them in sentences **Other:** making simple musical instruments

4.7 **Music from around the world**	Comparative adjectives: *smaller, not as … as* Past simple to describe events in the past *Going to* to describe future plans	Ordinal numbers: *first, second* Countries Geographical features: *mountains, island* Weather: *hot, cold, wet, windy, sunny*	**Speaking:** discussing the origin of pieces of music; expressing likes and dislikes; expressing opinions **Writing:** a postcard
4.8 **Write a song**	Depends on the model song	Music	**Listening and singing:** with focus on stress and rhythm **Writing:** the words to a song
4.9 **Mystery band**	Present simple Present continuous Prepositions of place: *behind, next to, between, in front of*	Clothes Musical instruments Roles in a band: *lead singer, guitarist*	**Reading:** for information **Speaking:** reporting on information gathered **Writing:** filling in a grid based on the information gathered
4.10 **The ELMAs – The English Language Music Awards**	Comparative and superlative adjectives: *the best … .* Possessive 's'	Recycling of vocabulary of music from previous activities	**Speaking:** discussing and making decisions; giving acceptance speeches **Writing:** nominations and acceptance speeches **Other:** designing and making an 'award'
4.11 **Make a 'fanzine'**	Revision of all structures covered in previous activities in the project	Revision of all vocabulary introduced and practised in previous activities in the project	Revision of all writing activities done in previous activities in the project Making illustrations, magazine covers, crosswords

4.1 Design a CD or cassette cover

LEVEL	**Elementary and above**
AGE GROUP	**11–13**
TIME	**60 minutes**

DESCRIPTION

In groups of two or three, the children invent a pop band: the name of the band, the type of music they play, the number of band members, and so on. They then design and illustrate a cassette cover or CD box. The finished work is displayed on the classroom walls.

LANGUAGE

Present simple to describe the pop band; likes and dislikes; introduction of more expressions to express likes/dislikes, for example: *I love … but I can't stand …* ; past simple to talk about when the band met; types of music; words and expressions to do with music.

SKILLS

Designing and drawing.

MATERIALS

Stiff paper or card; scissors; glue; crayons; coloured pens; old music magazines and newspapers (in any language, the children will only be using the pictures); examples of cassette covers and CD boxes, as many different covers as possible with a variety of illustrations.

PREPARATION

Ask the children to bring the cover or CD box of one of their singles or albums. You can also bring in examples of CD boxes and cassette covers of pop bands that the children will recognize, plus some examples of different types of bands. Try to cover a wide range of current music styles.

IN CLASS

1 Ask the children what kind of music they like. Write up some different kinds of music on the board.

2 Revise the language of likes and dislikes, and practise it by talking about the different types of music. Teach more unusual expressions, for example: *I can't stand …, I really love …, I'm keen on …* . Encourage the children to use the expressions with dramatic intonation.

3 Look at some of the CD covers together. If the children don't know the bands, tell them to guess the kind of music by looking at the illustrations on the covers.

4 Ask the children to think of current pop bands who play the different types of music written on the board, and write the names next to the words on the board.

5 Have a vote to decide which band is the class favourite. Get the children to write the name of their favourite band on a piece of paper, count all the votes, and announce the winner.

6 Write the name of the winning band on the board. Ask the children questions about the band.

What kind of music does the band play?
How many people are in the band?
When did the band start?
What was their first hit single?

7 Write the questions and answers in full sentences on the board, for example: *The band started in 1998.*

8 When all the questions and answers have been written on the board, look at the answers together. With the help of the children, write a paragraph about the band on a large piece of paper. Change *the band* to *it* where necessary. The children will be using the language from the biography in 4.2 'Invent a pop band'. Put the 'biography' on the wall.

9 Ask the children to draw or find a picture of the band.

10 Explain that the children are now going to create their own pop band, and that they are going to design a cover for their pop band's first hit CD or cassette.

11 Divide the children into groups of two or three. Write on the board the things the groups must decide.

---

the name of the pop band (an English name)
the type of music they play
the number of people in the band, their names, and ages (the members of the band must have English names)
the name of this record or CD (in English).

---

12 When the children have decided on the information about the band, they start to design their cassette or CD cover. They select a piece of card and cut it into the shape of a cassette cover or CD, depending on what they want to do. Explain to the children that they must include:
– the name of the pop band
– the name of the song
– illustrations to show the type of music.

13 The children can cut pictures from the music magazines that you have brought in. Tell the children to illustrate both sides of the cassette or CD cover and encourage them to be imaginative. Show them the examples you have brought in. Give the activity a time limit of 20 minutes, or get them to finish for homework.

14 Display the finished designs on the wall.

FOLLOW-UP	**1** One child can describe an album cover, while the others listen and identify the illustration being described.

2 The children can copy the biography of the class's favourite pop band into their notebooks or files and find or draw a picture to illustrate it.

3 Many CD covers include folded paper inserts containing such information as a biography of the band, song lyrics, and pictures. The children could add some of these to their CD insert as they do the other activities in the project.

4.2 Invent a pop band

LEVEL	**Elementary and above**
AGE GROUP	**11–13**
TIME	**60 minutes**
DESCRIPTION	In groups of two or three, the children develop their ideas about the pop band they invented in activity 4.1 'Design a CD or cassette cover'. They write a biography and description of their band, illustrate it, and present it in poster form.
LANGUAGE	Vocabulary of music as in 4.1 'Design a CD or cassette cover'; revision of past simple to talk about specific dates and actions in the past; clothes and appearance.
SKILLS	Cutting and drawing; working co-operatively.
MATERIALS	Large sheets of coloured paper for posters; white paper to write on; glue; scissors; coloured pens and pencils; old music magazines and newspapers to cut up (in any language as the children will only be using the pictures).
PREPARATION	**1** Prepare the questions for steps 3 and 4.

2 You could write up the prompt questions and copy them for each group to work with.

IN CLASS

1 Children work in the same groups that they worked in for activity 4.1, 'Design a CD or cassette cover' (see step 11 in 4.1). Remind children of the work they did when designing their covers. Explain that they are now going to invent a history of their band.

2 Revise present and past simple for specific events in the past, by taking the example of the class's favourite pop band (see activity 4.1, step 6). Look at the biography of the band. Write up the questions on the board. Practise asking and answering them about the band.

What's the band called?
How many people are in the band?
When did they meet?

3 In their pairs or groups of three, tell the children to write their own band's biography by following the questions on the board. The answers to the questions make up the biography. Encourage the children to make notes together first, and to agree about their band.

4 Build on the questions you have asked about the favourite band. Take an individual member of the band and ask for a brief description of that person from the class.

What does she look like?
She is very tall and she has long red hair.

What kind of clothes does she wear?
She always wears long green dresses.

Do you know anything about her hobbies or interests?
She has a pet hippopotamus, called Saskia.

What is her role in the band?
She is the lead singer.

5 Write up the description on a large piece of paper, get the children to make suggestions.

6 Get the children to write descriptions of their own bands, using this description as a model. Each child in the group should choose a different person and write an individual description. The children can illustrate their work by cutting out pictures from music magazines and newspapers, and by drawing pictures and designs.

7 Display the descriptions and band biographies in poster form on the wall, along with the album cover design that the children made in activity 4.1. Give the children time to go around the class and read the other descriptions.

VARIATION

Step 6 can be completed as homework.

4.3   A day in the life of a pop star

LEVEL	**Elementary and above**
AGE GROUP	**11–13**
TIME	**60 minutes**
DESCRIPTION	The children talk about their own daily routines and then imagine what a 'normal' day would be like for one of the members of the band they have invented. They produce a cartoon strip describing 'A day in the life of …'.
LANGUAGE	Present simple for describing habitual actions: *I get up at …* ; adverbs of frequency: *usually, always, sometimes, every day* (the activity can still be done without them); *in the morning/afternoon/ evening*.
SKILLS	Drawing pictures and arranging them to make a comic strip; gluing.
MATERIALS	Coloured pens; paper; magazines for cutting up; glue; a camera (optional); photocopies of Worksheet 4.3.

PREPARATION

1 Prepare a way of demonstrating habitual/daily actions, either by using flashcards or miming actions.

2 Prepare a worksheet divided into six boxes, each with a clock face in the corner (Worksheet 4.3).

3 Prepare eight or nine pieces of paper for each group, each about ten cms square.

IN CLASS

1 Draw a clock face on the board, and change the hands so that the time is appropriate for each activity. Mime some everyday actions, for example, brushing your teeth. Write up model sentences on the board:

> *At 7 o'clock I have breakfast.*
> *At 8 o'clock I catch the bus to school.*

2 Ask individual children to come to the front of the class and mime other everyday actions for the class to guess. Introduce the adverbs of frequency at this stage, if you wish.

3 Ask the children to think about their daily routine, and complete their own worksheet.

4 Tell the children to compare their daily routines with a partner by asking and answering the question: *What do you (usually) do at … o'clock?* Tell them to change the time for each question.

5 Divide the children into pairs or groups of three and ask them to choose a member of the pop band they invented in activity 4.2 (if they haven't invented a pop band, they can choose a real pop star).

6 Ask them to agree on eight or nine activities that make up a typical day in the life of their pop star. Encourage them to use their imaginations and come up with a combination of routine and unusual activities. For example, their pop star may have an unusual pet to take for a walk every day. Tell them to write the routine in note form:

> *7 o'clock — breakfast — pet snake.*

7 Give out eight or nine pieces of paper to each group. Ask them to decide which person is going to describe which activities—they each do three or four. On each piece of paper they draw a picture (or glue on a picture from a magazine) to illustrate the activity, and write one or two sentences along the bottom.

At seven o'clock Zedd has breakfast with his pet snake.

8 When they have finished their squares, they glue them on to a large piece of paper in the correct order to make a comic strip showing 'A day in the life of …'.

9 Display the comic strips on the walls so that the children can circulate and read each other's. Later, the strips can be included in, or copied into, the 'fanzine' in activity 4.11.

VARIATION

If you can take and develop photographs, the children could act and photograph some of their or their pop star's habitual actions, instead of drawing them. They can then write the captions under each photograph.

FOLLOW-UP

The class choose the daily routine they like best from those produced in comic strip form. They then photograph the activities together as a class. Give each group the task of acting out one of the activities. Some dressing-up clothes and suitable props would be useful. They will have to find imaginative ways of taking the part of the pop star's pet for the camera!

4.4   Design an outfit for a pop star

LEVEL	**Elementary and above**
AGE GROUP	**11–13**
TIME	**60 minutes**
DESCRIPTION	The children make posters, and design an outfit for a member of a pop band. They label their posters and write short descriptions.
LANGUAGE	Present continuous to describe what someone is wearing; order of adjectives; clothes.
SKILLS	Making a collage; drawing; working co-operatively.
MATERIALS	A selection of pop and fashion magazines; optional: bring in some clothing for the children to look at—it is more interesting if the clothes are bizarre, perhaps something the children will think very old-fashioned; photocopies of Worksheet 4.4.

PREPARATION

1 Find some pictures of famous pop bands or ask the children to bring some pictures from home.

2 Make flashcards of clothing items, colours, and patterns, or use Worksheet 4.4.

3 Make a poster by cutting out a picture of a famous pop star and labelling the clothing (see worksheet).

4 Write a model description of the famous pop star on your poster. The children can use it as a guide.

IN CLASS

1 Revise/present vocabulary of clothing using flashcards and examples of clothing.

2 Revise/present, patterns, colours, and order of adjectives, using flashcards. Write some examples on the board.

3 Show the children your labelled poster (see illustration) and ask the children to give a description of the person. Write up the description on the board, for example: *He is wearing a black and white T-shirt.*

4 The children work on their own, or in pairs. Explain that they are going to design an outfit for a member of their pop band. The children can either draw a figure or make one, using pictures cut out of magazines and newspapers. Encourage the children to make unusual outfits. Get the children to stick their design on a large piece of paper to make a poster. The children then label their posters with the name of their pop star, and label the various items of clothing. Give a strict time limit, for example, 20 minutes.

5 Tell the children to write a short description of what their pop star is wearing, following the ideas on the board and on your poster. Glue the description to the poster too.

6 The children can display their posters on the wall along with their pop bands.

4.5 Fashion show

LEVEL	**Elementary and above**
AGE GROUP	**11–13**
TIME	**60 minutes**
DESCRIPTION	In groups, the children make an outfit for one member of the band.
LANGUAGE	Present continuous to describe what someone is wearing; clothes and accessories.
SKILLS	Working co-operatively.
MATERIALS	Lots of newspapers; cooking foil; large black or coloured plastic rubbish bags, or other suitable material; scissors; staplers and staples; sticky tape (enough for the class when divided into groups of four or five); a camera and film (optional).

PREPARATION

1 Divide the materials so that there is enough for each group.
2 Clear a space for each group to work in.

IN CLASS

1 Organize the class into groups of four or five.
2 Explain that each group has 30 minutes to make an outfit for one member of the band, using the materials provided. The children should fit the outfit straight on to the group member who is going to be dressed. Explain that there will be a prize for the best outfit, and that you will take a photograph of all the models at the end of the activity.
3 Give each group a pile of newspapers, cooking foil black or coloured rubbish bags, or other suitable material, sticky tape, staplers and staples, and scissors.
4 Give the children 30 minutes to dress their band member in their special designer outfit. Make the children work fast and keep to the time limit.
5 When all the groups have finished, explain that the group must now present the outfit to the class—the dressed member of the group will be asked to parade like a model while the group describe what they are wearing, for example: *Sarah is wearing a long black dress and tall hat designed by … .* Give the children five minutes to prepare what they are going to say.
6 Ask each 'model' to parade, while the group describes what he or she is wearing. Each person in the group must say at least one sentence. After all the groups have finished, take a photograph of each 'model'.
7 The children can vote for the best costume, or you can award the prize for the best costume.

FOLLOW-UP

When the photographs have been developed, the children can write a description of their pop star model.

4.6   Making music

LEVEL	**Elementary and above**
AGE GROUP	**11–13**
TIME	**60 minutes**
DESCRIPTION	The children listen to and identify sounds such as *bang, crash, rattle, twang.* They design and make a simple musical instrument and describe the sound it makes. They invent an 'English' sound of their own.
LANGUAGE	Onomatopoeic words, that is, words that 'make' the sound they describe, for example, The drum goes *bang*.
SKILLS	Identifying and talking about the 'special' words/sounds; 'creating' words and using them in sentences; making musical instruments out of discarded household items.
MATERIALS	Tins; boxes; bottles; plastic containers; balloons; cereal boxes; strong elastic bands; dried peas; beans; lentils; pasta; sand; stones; musical instruments you have prepared.

PREPARATION

1 Ask the children to bring as many of the materials listed above as they can—at least one day before you plan to do the activity.

2 Make some musical instruments: simple drums, rattles, or shakers, to illustrate the sounds and give the children an example of an instrument they can make.

IN CLASS

1 Explain about words that 'make a sound'. Give examples in the children's own language or, in a multilingual class, ask them the sound made by a slamming door in their own languages. Then say: *In English the word is 'bang'.*

2 Choose some sounds in English and demonstrate them:

Sound	Action
Bang	a slamming door or a bursting balloon
Splash	a picture of someone jumping into a pool
Tinkle	a tiny bell or a small object in a glass bottle
Rattle	several objects shaken in a tin
Twang	a rubber band or guitar string
Hiss	make a hissing sound like a snake

3 Get the children to match the instruments and the sounds.

4 In pairs or groups of three, ask the children to invent a 'sound word' in English. Help them to make the word sound 'English' if necessary. They can then demonstrate or describe their sound to the class. For example:

Smoosh	a heavy ball falling in sand goes smoosh.
Splinkle	rain falling on the roof makes a splinkly sound.

5 Show the children the instruments you have brought into class, and the materials that they can use to make their own instruments.

6 In their groups, the children design, on paper, a musical instrument that can be made from the materials in the classroom. Feed in ideas if necessary—see examples of instruments they can make. Check that the designs are practical (and safe!).

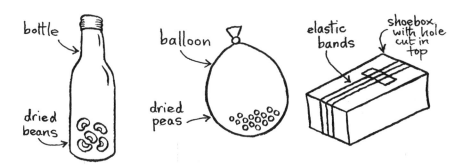

7 Let the children choose the materials and make the instrument they have designed.

8 Ask the children to give their instrument a name. It could be a blend of the names of two real instruments, for example: *drum* + *maraca* = *drumaca*. They then describe the sound it makes by using a word already mentioned or by inventing a special one.

9 The groups demonstrate their instruments and describe them.

This is our drumaca. It goes bang and splinkle.
Our drumaca makes a banging and splinkly sound.

VARIATION

If you don't have sufficient materials for all the children to make instruments, you can make one or two together as a class, chosen from the designs drawn by the children. You can then have a competition to see which group can invent the best name and most effective 'sound word' to describe the sound the instrument makes.

FOLLOW-UP

After the class have written their song in activity 4.9, they can perform the song using their instruments. If they don't write a song, any song in English can be accompanied by the children playing the instruments.

4.7 Music from around the world

LEVEL

Elementary and above

AGE GROUP

11–13

TIME

60 minutes

DESCRIPTION

The children listen to a selection of pieces of music from around the world. They guess where the music comes from and talk about what they know about these countries. The children write a postcard home, imagining that they are a member of the pop band that they have created in activity 4.2.

LANGUAGE

Comparative adjectives; past simple to describe past events; *going to* to describe future plans; ordinal numbers: *1st, 2nd, 3rd*, and so on; vocabulary associated with the countries: *large, mountainous, an island*, and so on; weather.

SKILLS

Speculating on the origin of pieces of music; expressing likes and dislikes; expressing opinions.

MATERIALS

Five short pieces of music from around the world. The pieces of music should be as varied as possible. Each piece should be about one or two minutes long. Good examples would be: Scottish bagpipes, Russian dancing music, African drums and singing, or Aboriginal didgeridoo music; a large map of the world for reference; coloured tape and board pins; blank cards the size of postcards.

PREPARATION

1 Record the music.
2 Make a set of ten cards, each with the name of a different country on, including the five countries where the music extracts come from (five of the countries will not match your music, and five will). You will need one set of cards for each pair of children.

IN CLASS

1 Put the children into pairs. Explain to the children that you are going to play them some music from around the world. Explain that when they listen you want them to see if they can guess which country the music comes from. Give each pair a set of ten cards. Check that they know where each country is on the map.
2 Play each music extract twice, and give the children time to discuss, in pairs, where they think the music comes from. They arrange their cards in order as they listen to the music.
3 Play the extracts again. Stop after each extract and ask them if they liked the music. Encourage them to express their opinions. Ask them where they think the music comes from. Write the country up on the board and ask the children what they know about that country, for example: Scotland—there are a lot of mountains and castles. There is a monster in Loch Ness. Russia—it is very cold in the north of Russia. There is a lot of snow and ice and many big forests.
4 Compare some of the aspects of the various countries and write the comparisons on the board. *Russia is larger than Scotland. It is hotter in Australia than in Scotland.*
5 Explain that you want the children to imagine that they are a member of their pop band. They are visiting these five countries on a world tour.

6 Working either individually, or in pairs, ask the children to decide which countries they are going to visit and in which order. Together, they decide a route and mark it on the map with coloured tape and pins, or with pen.

7 Explain that the pop stars are now in the third country that they are visiting and they are going to write a postcard home to the editor of their 'fanzine' magazine telling their fans about their world tour so far, and where they are going next.

8 Write the postcard on the board, get ideas from the class. Include the past simple, some comparatives, and *going to* for the future, for example:

> Last week we went to Russia. We did a concert in St Petersburg. It was very cold, but Scotland was colder! We did an outside concert in Edinburgh and it was freezing! Now we are in Africa, in Zimbabwe. It is very hot and very beautiful here. I want to see some elephants. Next week we are going to Australia. Australia is not as hot as Africa. We are going to visit a surfing beach. Our last concert is in South America on 6 November ... .

9 The children copy the words from the board on to their blank postcard. The children can draw or stick a picture on the front of the postcard. Display the finished postcards around the map.

FOLLOW-UP

Some of the children might like to contribute a longer letter to their fans, describing their concert tour, for the 'fanzine' activity, 4.11.

4.8 Write a song

LEVEL

Elementary and above

AGE GROUP

11–13

TIME

60 minutes

DESCRIPTION

In groups, the children create a song to be performed by the pop band they have created. The finished songs can be published in the 'fanzine' (activity 4.11), and performed by the children.

LANGUAGE

Focus on stress and rhythm patterns; any appropriate language known to the children. As this is a creative writing activity, the children will use whatever language they choose, but it would be useful to encourage them to recycle grammar and vocabulary from previous activities in the project.

SKILLS   Imagination.

MATERIALS   The words of some simple English songs that are already familiar to
                        the children; paper and pencils or pens.

PREPARATION   The children will need to be familiar with a song in English that has
                        an easily remembered melody. In a monolingual class, a song in
                        their own language could be used—all they need to do is 'borrow'
                        the tune.

IN CLASS   1 Sing a simple English song that you have taught the children.
                        2 Write the words of the song on the board. If it is too long, just
                           write up the first verse, or the chorus.

She'll be comin' round the mountain

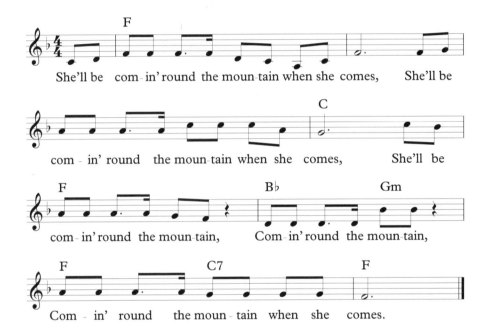

                        3 Ask them to look at the words on the board. Help them to count
                           the number of syllables in each line. For the song above there are:

                           Line 1—11 syllables
                           Line 2—11 syllables
                           Line 3—8 syllables
                           Line 4—6 syllables
                           Line 5—9 syllables

                           She'll/ be/ com/in/ round/ the/ moun/tain/ when/ she/ comes/
                           She'll/ be/ com/in/ round/ the/ moun/tain/ when/ she/ comes/
                           She'll/ be/ com/in/ round/ the/ moun/tain/
                           Com/in/ round/ the/ moun/tain/
                           Com/in/ round/ the/ moun/tain/ when/ she/ comes/

                        4 Now ask them to clap in time to the music as you/they sing it, and
                           to count the number of claps (beats) per line. Each clap or beat
                           coincides with a stressed syllable. For this song there are:

Line 1—6 beats
Line 2—6 beats
Line 3—4 beats
Line 4—3 beats
Line 5—5 beats

She'll/ be/ com/in/ round/ the/ moun/tain/ when/ she/ comes/
She'll/ be/ com/in/ round/ the/ moun/tain/ when/ she/ comes/
She'll/ be/ com/in/ round/ the/ moun/tain/
Com/in/ round/ the/ moun/tain
Com/in/ round/ the/ moun/tain/ when/ she/ comes/

This is a simple way to introduce the children to the stress-timed nature of English.

5 Ask the children, in groups of two or three, to write their own version of the song by changing some or all of the words, but keeping the same grammatical structures, melody, and rhythm. Do an example together on the board before asking them to do one in their groups.

> We'll be playing hip hop music in our band
> We'll be playing hip hop music in our band
> We'll be playing hip hop music
> Playing hip hop music
> Playing hip hop music in our band

6 Monitor the activity and give help if necessary. Some groups may produce more than one verse. When the children have all finished their verses, you or they can write the words on the board, or on large pieces of paper so that the class can sing them together.

7 The children can write their verses, with suitable illustrations, for activity 4.11 'Make a fanzine'.

4.9 Mystery band

LEVEL

Elementary and above

AGE GROUP

11–13

TIME

45 minutes

DESCRIPTION

The children are given a picture of a pop band. They have to discover the names of the people in the pop band and their roles in the band. In pairs, the children read and gather information from sentences stuck up around the room. They fill in their answers on a grid (see photocopiable Worksheet 4.9).

LANGUAGE

Present simple; present continuous; prepositions of place: *behind, next to, between, in front of*; clothes; musical instruments; roles in the band: *lead singer, guitarist*.

SKILLS

Assessing information and reporting back.

MATERIALS

Information about the band photocopied on to card, and cut into strips (see below); a photocopy of the picture of the pop band for each pair (see Worksheet 4.9); a photocopy of the answer sheet for each pair; some pictures of pop bands—make sure there are several members in the band.

PREPARATION

1 Photocopy the information sentences below and cut them into strips.

2 Stick the strips up around the classroom.

Joe Best plays the guitar
Ted is wearing black and white striped trousers
Joe Best is standing between Karen and Rob
Rob is standing behind the microphone
Rob is the lead singer
Seb is wearing a black t-shirt
Jess is standing next to Seb
Jess is shorter than Seb
Charlie plays the keyboard
Karen plays the keyboard
Charlie is standing behind Karen
Lucinda is standing next to Karen
Sometimes Jess plays the trumpet
Everyone in the band sings

Photocopiable © Oxford University Press

IN CLASS

1 Put a picture of one of the pop bands you have brought in, on the board. Ask the students to name the members of the band, and revise present continuous and vocabulary for clothes by asking the students what the pop stars are wearing. Write the answers on the board: *She is wearing a black and white T-shirt and red trousers.*

2 Revise/present prepositions of place by looking at the picture, for example: *Jack is standing behind Paulo. Georgia is next to Jack.*

3 Put the children in pairs and, if possible, give each pair a different picture of a pop band. Ask the children to write five sentences about the picture together, using the prepositions you have practised on the board.

4 Give each pair the photocopied picture of the pop band and grid to fill in. Explain that they can find out all the answers by reading the information which is written up around the room.

5 Allow the children to move around the room in their pairs, reading the slips of card on the wall and finding out the information.

6 When most of the children have filled in their grids, check the answers.

7 Tell the children to work out the name of the band by using the last letters of the names of the band members. The answer should be BEST BAND.

4.10 The ELMAs—The English Language Music Awards

LEVEL

Elementary and above

AGE GROUP

11–13

TIME

90 minutes

DESCRIPTION

The children prepare and take part in an award ceremony, similar to 'The Oscars' or the musical equivalent 'The Grammies'. They decide on the categories of awards, write nominations, form a panel of judges to decide on the winners in each category, make the awards', and perform an awards ceremony at which acceptance speeches are made.

LANGUAGE

Comparative and superlative adjectives; possessive 's'; vocabulary from previous activities in the project.

SKILLS

Discussion and making joint decisions; designing and making an 'award'.

MATERIALS

Pieces of card to write nominees' names on; envelopes for the winning nominations; card; gold paint; silver or gold foil; glue; ribbons, and other decorations to make the awards or medals.

PREPARATION

1 Ask the children to collect silver/gold wrappings from chocolate bars, and bring in ribbons.

2 To explain the context of the activity, show the class photographs or posters of award-winning films, actors, or singers. A picture of the world famous 'Oscar' statuette would be useful.

3 Find a video clip of any kind of award ceremony (optional).

IN CLASS

1 Find out what the children know about awards and award ceremonies. In low-level, monolingual classes some of this background could be discussed in the children's own language.

2 Show any pictures or video clips of award ceremonies. Introduce the idea of the English Language Music Awards—'The ELMAs', and explain that they are going to have their own award ceremony.

3 Present or revise comparatives and superlatives. If the language is new to the class, you can restrict it for this activity to *better* and *best*. Introduce the language by giving the class a questionnaire about their own preferences. For example:

Which is the best pop band in the world?
Who is the best singer?
Are the … better than … ? (choose groups known to the class)

4 Ask the questions and get a range of answers. Be prepared for differences of opinion. Ask the children to write the questions and their own answers in their notebooks.

5 Divide the children into groups of three or four and ask them to think about five categories (or kinds) of awards they would like to have at their ELMAs. These should be based on previous activities from the project. For example: the ELMA for best record or CD design, best song, best musical instrument made in class.

   You may want to suggest categories to include a recognition of the different types of work done by the children for the project.

6 When the categories have been decided, write them on the board and give the children time to discuss in their groups who they want to vote for in each category. To make it more varied, you can tell the children that they can't nominate the same person/people for more than one category. Ask them to write down their decisions. For example: *The best cassette cover is Maria and Carlo's.*

7 Collect the votes in. Work out who has won each award. Write the name of the winners in each category on a piece of paper and place it in an envelope.

8 While you are working out the winners, the children design the actual awards. Give each group one award to design and produce. Give them some ideas—the best CD cover could be in the shape of a cassette or CD, for example. They can make their awards out of thick card, cut them out, cover them in gold or silver foil, or paint them and decorate them so they are ready to give out at the awards ceremony. They may also want to make 'medals' to give to each winner.

9 The award ceremony: each group can announce the winners and present the award in the category for which they have designed the actual award. Stage this like an 'Oscar' ceremony. Prepare the children by practising phrases such as *And the winner is … , The award for best … goes to … .* Winning groups can collect their awards and make acceptance speeches. Before the ceremony practise such phrases as *I'm thrilled/delighted/very happy to win this award, I would like to thank … for their help.*

VARIATION	If you have a camera, photograph the award ceremony for the 'fanzine' (activity 4.11) to display on the classroom wall. The children can then write the captions for the photographs, for example: *At the ELMAs Richard, Keiko, and Elisabeth won the award for the best performance of an English song.*

4.11 Make a fanzine

LEVEL	**Elementary and above**
AGE GROUP	**11–13**
TIME	**As long as you wish to spend on it**
DESCRIPTION	The children make a collection of the work done during the music project and present it in the form of a magazine or 'fanzine' which can be displayed in class, or photocopied and a copy given to each child.
LANGUAGE	Revision of all structures and vocabulary covered in previous activities in this project.
SKILLS	Creative imagination in making illustrations, magazine covers, crosswords, and so on.
MATERIALS	Sheets of paper (A4 size or A3 size folded) on which the finished work will be mounted, these sheets can then either be photocopied or compiled into a class magazine; copies of pop magazines for the children to look at for ideas.
IN CLASS	1 Pieces of work for the fanzine can be collected as the children work on the project, or you can spend several lessons at the end of the project collecting the work together and presenting it attractively. You can be the editor, making the final decisions about what is to be included, and how much you want to correct the work. You will probably only want to include one or two examples of each type of item—usually the best, but you must make sure that all the children contribute something. As most of the contents have been prepared in earlier activities, the articles put in the magazine will be the 'second draft' as you correct the work when necessary.

2 Show the children some examples of pop magazines for ideas on content and style, how to write the headlines and the captions for the pictures, and how to write a contents list. Don't forget to include a list of all the contributors (everyone in the class) with perhaps a photo or drawing of each person next to their name.

3 You need to decide, together, on the design and layout of the fanzine. You can spend part of an activity designing a front and back cover, or set the task for homework after discussion in class. The class can vote on the best cover to have on their fanzine.

4 Try to have the magazine copied so that each child has one to take home. Be prepared for the fact that photographs do not copy very well—they are best done on a light setting on the photocopier. If you have access to a colour photocopier the end-product will be much better—but expensive! It might be possible to colour copy the cover only.

VARIATION

In a class of higher-level children you can divide the class into groups and let each group put together their own magazine, using examples of their own work. You can suggest items to be included from the list below.

Items which can be included in the fanzine

4.1   A selection of the children's designs for the CD boxes and cassette covers. Some of the children could write a short review of the 'newly released' albums.

4.2   A selection of the pop band biographies, with pictures of the bands.

4.3   A selection of the comic strips describing a day in the life of their chosen pop star.

4.4   A selection of the descriptions of the pop stars and their clothes, with pictures.

4.5   A report of the fashion show with photographs of the children wearing their costumes, and descriptions of the outfits.

4.6   A selection of the designs for the musical instruments, with their names and a short description of the sounds they make.

4.7   Some of the children's postcards from around the world. Longer letters to their fans about their trip. Copies of the maps showing the route.

4.8   The words of some of the songs written by the class.

4.9   The picture of the mystery band, the 'clues', and the 'answers'.

4.10 An article describing the award ceremony with a list of the categories and the winners.

ADDITIONAL

– Letters from fans written to the pop bands asking questions about the band, responses from the band members.
– A crossword based on words to do with music, clothes, or countries.
– A word search based on words to do with music, clothes, or countries.
– Pop star profiles including name, age, star sign, favourite food, favourite animal, and so on.

Project 5
Fantasy island

Description of the project

In this project the students create a fantasy island and explore different aspects of life on the island.

Main products of each activity

On completion of the project the class will have produced/achieved the following:

5.1 Map your island
A large wall map of the island or a three-dimensional model of the island

5.2 Fly the flag
A flag for the island

5.3 Fantasy creatures
Posters of fantasy creatures
Description of the creatures' habitats and habits

5.4 Ideal homes
Posters or three-dimensional models of houses
Description of houses

5.5 Celebrity guests
An invitation

5.6 Tour of the island
An itinerary for a trip around the island
A photo montage

5.7 Making money
Banknotes and coins
A written biography

5.8 Fantasy holidays
A travel guide

5.9 Elect a president
An election manifesto
News reports
An election poster and slogan

5.10 Fantasy island poetry book
A poetry book

5.11 Island news
A class newspaper or magazine

Language and skills

Activity	Grammatical and functional	Vocabulary	Skills
5.1 **Map your island**	Present simple Giving directions	Points of the compass Geographical features	**Speaking:** making suggestions; giving directions **Writing:** labels **Other:** designing; drawing; cutting
5.2 **Fly the flag**	… *represents* …	Colours Shapes Geographical features Nationalities	**Listening** to a short description **Writing:** description of a flag **Speaking:** giving a presentation **Other:** designing; drawing; painting
5.3 **Fantasy creatures**	Present simple for describing habits and habitats *Has got*	Animals Body parts Biological terms: *mammal* and so on Animal habitats	**Speaking:** describing an animal; asking questions **Writing:** a description of an animal **Other:** designing; drawing or painting
5.4 **Ideal homes**	Present simple Passive: *is/are made of*	Geographical features Climate Houses and rooms Types of buildings Building materials	**Listening** to a description of a house **Writing:** description of a house **Other:** designing; drawing or painting
5.5 **Celebrity guests**	Inviting	Adjectives for describing people	**Writing:** an invitation **Speaking:** describing a person **Other:** cutting and gluing
5.6 **Tour of the island**	Present simple for itineraries	Places Times	**Writing:** an itinerary **Speaking:** describing an itinerary **Other:** cutting and gluing; planning
5.7 **Making money**	Past simple Past perfect	Numbers Jobs	**Reading:** short biographies **Writing:** a biography **Speaking:** making suggestions; expressing ideas; giving a presentation **Other:** designing; drawing; cutting

5.8 **Fantasy holidays**	Present simple Present continuous Imperatives Modals: *can, must* Comparative and superlative adjectives	Geographical features Tourist information	**Reading:** holiday brochures **Speaking:** negotiating **Writing:** information for a travel brochure
5.9 **Elect a president**	Past simple Past perfect Future: *will, going to* Present perfect Reported speech	Newspaper headlines Elections	**Writing:** short news reports; a manifesto **Speaking:** making a speech; asking questions
5.10 **Fantasy island poetry book**	Second conditional: *If I were … I would/ could …; … is like …*	Vocabulary from previous activities in the project	**Writing:** poetry. **Speaking:** reciting poetry
5.11 **Island news**	Revision of: Present tenses Past tenses Future tenses Reported speech	Vocabulary introduced in previous activities in the project	**Reading:** newpapers **Writing:** newspaper articles; advertisements

5.1 Map your island!

LEVEL	**Intermediate and above**
AGE GROUP	12–14
TIME	**90 minutes**

DESCRIPTION

The children design an island on which the class project will be based. The children make a large wall map of the island and it is put up on the classroom wall. They can also make small maps of the island for their own files.

LANGUAGE

Present simple; describing geographical features and places; points of the compass; giving directions.

SKILLS

Designing; drawing; cutting.

MATERIALS

A selection of atlases; reference books showing pictures of islands and various geographical features such as mountain ranges, volcanoes, swamps, forests, jungles, deserts, and so on; large sheets of paper; coloured pens and pencils; paint and paint brushes, if you wish to paint the island.

PREPARATION

1 Collect or draw a set of pictures showing geographical features, for example: a mountain range, a swamp, a desert, a waterfall, and a forest. Number the pictures.
2 Stick the pictures around the room.
3 Stick some large pieces of paper together and draw an interesting island shape on it. Stick it on the wall.

IN CLASS

1 Show the class the outline of the island you have drawn, and tell them that they are going to add features to it. Get the class to choose a name for the island.
2 Put the children into pairs. Give each child a list of the words, and tell them to walk around the room and match the words to the correct pictures.
3 Give them the answers and practise saying the words.
4 Divide the children into groups of four or five. Give each group some reference books and an atlas. Tell the children to make a list of the features they want to include on their island and suggest names for them, for example: *Blue River, Wild Wood, Snowy Mountains*. They can suggest additional features they have found in the reference books.
5 Each group tells the class about their ideas, while you make a list on the board. When you have listed all the features, the class decides which they would most like to include on the island.
6 Teach/revise the points of the compass: *north, south, east*, and *west*.
7 The class decides where the geographical features are situated on the island, for example: *There is a mountain range in the north called The Jagged Teeth Mountains*. Write the suggestions in pencil on the map.

8 Tell the children to choose one or more of the geographical features to draw, colour, cut out, and label. Glue the drawing and label on to the map in the position marked by pencil. Add rivers to link up the lakes and waterfalls. Add the name of the island, a compass, and a measuring scale.

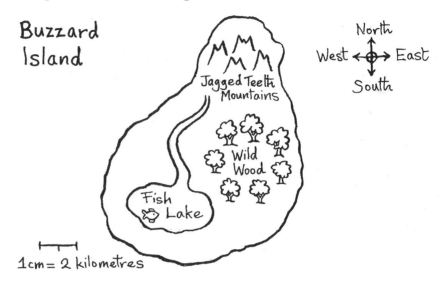

VARIATION	Instead of, or in addition to, the poster, the children can make a three-dimensional model of the island using chicken wire and papier mâché, or cardboard, egg cartons, and so on.
FOLLOW-UP	As the children complete other activities in the project, they can add other pictures to the map of the island, for example: animals, houses, people, shops, and so on.

5.2 Fly the flag

LEVEL	**Intermediate and above**
AGE GROUP	**12–14**
TIME	**30–40 minutes**
DESCRIPTION	The children design a flag for their fantasy island, which is displayed on the classroom wall. They explain to the rest of the class what the different colours and symbols on the flag represent.
LANGUAGE	... *represents* ... ; colours; shapes; geographical features: *river, mountain*, and so on; nationalities.
SKILLS	Designing; drawing; painting.
MATERIALS	Large sheets of white paper (at least A3 size); paints, crayons, or felt tip pens.
PREPARATION	Collect or make examples of flags.

IN CLASS

1 Revise vocabulary for colours and basic shapes: *square, rectangle, circle, triangle, star, crescent, stripes.*

2 Show the children examples of flags (their own, the flags of English-speaking countries, and so on) from a reference book or drawn on the board. The children themselves may be able to draw flags they know on the board. This stage could be presented as a quiz, where the children try to recognize the flags of different countries.

3 Put the children into groups of three or four, and tell them that they are going to design a flag of their own for the fantasy island they created in the previous activity.

4 Give them an example of what you want them to do by showing them a well-known flag and explaining what its design and colours represent. The 'Union Jack' of the UK would be a good example to use, as its three separate crosses represent the patron saints of England, Wales, and Scotland combined. Give them language such as: *The red cross represents St George who is the patron saint of England. Blue is the colour of St Andrew of Scotland.*

5 Practise the structure … *represents* … . The children can guess what the symbols on the flags represent, for example: *I think the red circle on the Japanese flag represents the sun.*

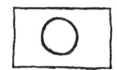

6 Tell the children to design, draw, and paint one flag per group, thinking carefully about what each colour or symbol represents.

7 In their groups, the children discuss how they will describe and explain their design to the rest of the class. They write a short description.

8 The children then display their flags on the classroom wall. Everyone walks around, looking at each other's designs.

9 Get each group to talk to the rest of the class about their flag. Display their written descriptions alongside the flags on the wall.

10 The whole class votes for the flag they would like to adopt to represent their fantasy island.

VARIATION

1 If you have enough reference books/encyclopaedias available, the children can do their own research into flags of different nations and their origins.

2 The class as a whole decide on a design and colour which they all draw in their exercise books. Then, in groups, the children think of an explanation for each colour and symbol.

The gold represents the golden beaches.
The blue is the blue sea all around the island.
The white circle is a symbol of peace.
The red is for the red-hot sun.

5.3 Fantasy creatures

LEVEL	**Intermediate and above**
AGE GROUP	**12–14**
TIME	**60 minutes**
DESCRIPTION	The children design a fantasy creature to inhabit their island. They make posters of each animal and write about the animal's habits, its habitat, the way it rears its young, if it is endangered and why, and so on.
LANGUAGE	Present simple for describing habits; *has got*; body parts; animals; biological terms: *mammal, reptile, amphibian, insect, bird*; animal habitats: *nest, hole, warren, den, burrow*, and so on.
SKILLS	Designing; drawing or painting.
MATERIALS	Reference books, including pictures of different animals from around the world, and their habitats; books with pictures of fantasy animals such as unicorns, dragons, sea monsters, and satyrs; large sheets of paper; colour pens and pencils; Worksheet 5.3.
PREPARATION	Select some pictures of unusual animals, and some fantasy animals to show the children. Photocopy Worksheet 5.3 on the types of animals: reptiles, mammals, and so on.

IN CLASS

1 Explain that the children are going to design some fantasy creatures to live on their island.

2 Introduce the vocabulary for the types of animals, for example, *mammals* and *reptiles*.

3 Do the worksheet: the children match the words to the pictures.

4 Introduce the vocabulary for where the animals live: *nest, hole*, and so on, and ask the children for suggestions about what the creatures eat: *fruit, insects, people!* Write up the vocabulary on the board with pictures you have drawn or collected, and practise saying the words.

5 Tell the children to work individually, or in pairs, and design an animal.

6 Ask the children to make a large poster of their animal. They should include pictures of the food the animal eats, and the kind of place it lives in.

7 Get the children to write a description of their creature. They should include information about where it lives, its food, and its habits.

8 In pairs, the children take it in turns to answer questions about their creature, for example: *What does it like to eat? How many legs has it got?* before they display their poster.

FOLLOW-UP

The children could make their work into a 'Fantasy Island Natural History Information Guide' for visitors to the island who are interested in wildlife.

5.4   Ideal homes

LEVEL

Intermediate and above

AGE GROUP

12–14

TIME

30–40 minutes (longer if model houses are made)

DESCRIPTION

The children discuss, design, and produce their ideal home for their fantasy island. The finished houses can be in poster form or three-dimensional models, depending on how long you wish to spend on the activity and what materials you have available.

LANGUAGE

Passive: … *is/are made of* … ; revision of vocabulary used to describe geographical features and climate; rooms and furniture; types of houses; building materials.

SKILLS

Designing; drawing or painting.

MATERIALS

Large sheets of white paper (at least A3 size); paints, crayons or felt pens; materials for model-making, if appropriate: glue, scissors, card, and paint.

PREPARATION

Collect reference books or pictures showing different kinds of houses and homes, for example: *igloos, wigwams,* or *log cabins.*

IN CLASS

1 Show the children examples of different houses and homes from a reference book, or from pictures and posters. This stage could be presented as a quiz, where the children try to recognize different kinds of houses from various parts of the world.

2 Discuss why houses can be so different from each other (because of the climate, and so on), and elicit the kinds of materials used to construct them.

3 Elicit the names of different rooms in a house and other useful vocabulary such as doors and windows, and write them on the board.

4 Give the children the names of any other useful materials and add them to the list on the board.

5 Teach/revise the structures … *is/are made of* … by talking about the different houses.

6 Tell the children that they are going to design a house for the inhabitants of the fantasy island they have created. Decide, or let the children choose, whether they will work individually, in pairs, or small groups.

7 Do the first example together as a class on the board. Elicit/give language.

> This house is called a bubbloo. It is an igloo made of glass that changes colour according to the temperature outside. It floats above the ground, so it can be built anywhere. Inside there are six rooms. One of the rooms is called the 'dream room'. You can go inside and choose a dream you would like to have.

8 Ask the children to design, draw, and paint their houses, illustrating both the inside and the outside. Get them to label the different parts and rooms.
9 When they have finished their drawing, they find another person, pair, or group to show it to, and describe its various features.
10 When the children have all had a chance to show each other their houses, they write up their descriptions, using the model provided earlier by you to help them. Display the drawings and descriptions on the walls.

FOLLOW-UP

If there is time, and suitable materials are available, the class can select one or two of the houses to turn into three-dimensional models.

5.5 Celebrity guests

LEVEL

Intermediate and above

AGE GROUP

12–14

TIME

30 minutes

DESCRIPTION

The children choose a famous person, dead or alive, real or imaginary, who they would like to invite to visit their island and write an invitation to their guest.

LANGUAGE

Adjectives used to describe a person; writing an invitation.

SKILLS	Cutting and gluing.
MATERIALS	Magazines which include pictures of famous people which the children can cut out (or set them a task for homework—to find a photo of their favourite person and bring it to the lesson). Stiff card.
PREPARATION	Choose the guest you are going to invite and make some notes about why you chose this person.
IN CLASS	1 Tell the children that they are going to invite their favourite pop star/actor/sport star to visit the island.

2 Let them decide whether they want to work in pairs or individually.

3 In pairs or individually, get them to choose who to invite, and look for a picture of their guest to cut out.

4 Tell the children about your guest, referring to the notes you have prepared.

5 Ask the children to think about why they have chosen their guest, and make written notes.

6 Put the children into groups of six or eight. Tell them to take it in turns to tell the others who they have chosen and why, using their notes

7 Write the invitation to your guest on the board, or use a photocopied example. The children then write an invitation for their guest and decorate it.

5.6 Tour of the island

LEVEL	**Intermediate and above**
AGE GROUP	**12–14**
TIME	**45–60 minutes**
DESCRIPTION	The children plan and write up an itinerary for the guest they invited to the island in 5.5. They then record their itinerary on cassette.
LANGUAGE	Present simple.

SKILLS

Planning and writing an itinerary; using a cassette recorder.

MATERIALS

Photographs of the children which can be cut up; travel brochures and magazines.

PREPARATION

1 Ask the children to bring in a photograph of themselves.

2 Prepare an example of an itinerary.

IN CLASS

1 The children work in the same pairs as in 5.5, or individually.

2 Ask the children to plan a tour of the island they created in 5.1 for their guest. The tour can include seeing some of the creatures from 5.3, and visiting the island home created in 5.4.

3 Get them to write up the itinerary and decorate it with pictures they have drawn, or with photographs cut out from magazines.

4 The children make a souvenir photograph of themselves and their guest. They glue the pictures of themselves and their guest on to a card, to look like a picture taken of the two of them together. The children then display their souvenir photograph with the itinerary and invitation.

5 They can then record their itinerary onto cassette so that it can be listened to while following the route on the map of the island. Below is an example of a recorded itinerary.

At nine o'clock we leave the hotel and go by bus to the famous Walampi Volcano and Lake. If you are lucky you may see the volcano erupting. Then, at twelve o'clock we visit a typical island home which is by the side of the lake. Here we have lunch—fish caught in the lake and delicious island fruit.

FOLLOW-UP 1

The children write a diary entry describing the day they spent with their famous guest on the island.

FOLLOW-UP 2

The children interview each other—one is the reporter and one the famous guest—and write articles for the island newspaper.

5.7 Making money

LEVEL

Intermediate and above

AGE GROUP

12–14

TIME

50–60 minutes

DESCRIPTION

The children devise and design a system of currency for their fantasy island. The results can be displayed in their notebooks, or on the classroom walls. Copies of the banknotes and coins can be made for use when you do shop or restaurant role plays.

LANGUAGE

Past simple and past perfect; numbers; jobs.

SKILLS

Giving a presentation; designing; drawing; cutting.

MATERIALS

Paper and scissors; pencils; crayons or felt pens; cardboard to make coins.

PREPARATION

1 If possible, bring in examples of coins and banknotes from a variety of different countries. The children may have some foreign coins or notes if they have been to other countries.
2 Bring in some short biographies of famous people: encyclopaedias and the Internet are useful places to look.

IN CLASS

1 Revise narrative past tenses by reading short biographies of a national hero from the children's own country, or an English-speaking one. This could be a famous politician, sports star, scientist, or anyone whose life would be of interest to the class. Choose a simple text with little or no unknown vocabulary, for example: *Neil Armstrong was the first man to walk on the moon. Before becoming an astronaut he had worked as a pilot in the airforce.* Give each child a copy of the text.
2 Get the children to read the text individually and answer any questions they have about vocabulary.
3 Divide the children into small groups. Ask them to 'create' a national hero for their fantasy island, and write a paragraph describing this person's life. Encourage them to use the narrative past tenses you revised.
4 Tell them that they will be designing their own banknotes for their island, and incorporating their hero's portrait into the design. The hero could be the celebrity from activity 5.5 and the notes designed

to commemorate their visit. Give the children time to study the real banknotes. Ask them, in their groups, to make a list of all the features a real banknote has so that they can make their work look as 'authentic' as possible. Write these points on the board.

5 As a class, decide what the currency is to be called. For example, it could be named after the island itself. If the island were called 'Dunwood Island' after the founder Patrick Burdun and the first President Agnes Woodford, then the currency could be the 'Dunwood'.

6 Decide how much a 'Dunwood' is worth. Once the class has agreed, give each group a note of a different value to design. You could ask some groups to design coins.

7 The children discuss, design, and draw their banknotes and coins. Remind them that they need to do both sides of the notes/coins and include the portrait of the national hero. When finished they can cut the notes/coins out.

8 Tell the groups to decide how they will describe and explain their design to the rest of the class.

9 Get them to display their banknotes and coins on their tables or on the classroom walls. Everyone can walk around and look at them.

10 In groups, the children talk to the rest of the class about their notes. Their explanation, together with the life history of their national hero, can be written up and displayed alongside the banknotes on the classroom wall.

FOLLOW-UP

Copy the coins and banknotes, and use them in restaurant and shop role plays.

5.8 Fantasy holidays

LEVEL

Intermediate and above

AGE GROUP

12–14

TIME

60 minutes or more, depending on how detailed you want the guide to be

DESCRIPTION

The children design and write a travel guide for their fantasy island. They present it in the form of a brochure or booklet. The guide can include things such as a description of the hotels and guest houses, island cuisine, leisure activities, climate, flora and fauna, the people, geographical features, and exciting day trips. The children use travel guides and brochures as examples.

LANGUAGE

Present simple and continuous; imperatives; modals; comparative and superlative adjectives; travel language.

SKILLS

Negotiating and making decisions.

MATERIALS	Travel brochures for children to read and get pictures from; white paper to make the brochure; glue; scissors; coloured pens and pencils.
PREPARATION	Bring in a selection of various types of travel brochures and posters for the children to look at and cut up.

IN CLASS

1 Put the children into groups and get them to look through travel brochures to see how they are organized, and to see the language used in the brochures, for example: *Swim with the dolphins at Emerald Bay; Ride on an elephant through the Wild Wood.*

2 Tell them they are going to write a guide for their island. Brainstorm a selection of topic areas which they could include in their guides, for example: leisure activities on the islands; places to stay; wildlife viewing; what to bring on your visit. Put the topics on the board.

3 Let the children choose whether they want to work in pairs or in threes.

4 Get each group to choose which topic or topics they would like to work on for the guide.

5 The children write the text and draw pictures, or use photographs cut from holiday brochures or travel guides. Monitor the work being produced by the groups. Make suggestions, and correct the language as appropriate. Ask each group to produce a good final copy.

6 Put all the sections together to make a brochure.

FOLLOW-UP

The guide can be used for a reading exercise. Let the children read each other's contributions, and then they could give feedback.

VARIATION 1

The class work on individual mini guides, with each group covering all the topics.

VARIATION 2

The class work on individual guides over several lessons and the language input is much more focused, that is, there is a lesson on an area of grammar or vocabulary, followed by a part of the guide which includes that area of language.

5.9 Elect a president

LEVEL	**Intermediate and above**
AGE GROUP	12–14
TIME	**90 minutes**
DESCRIPTION	Some of the children form political parties, write a manifesto, and make speeches, while the other children, as newspaper reporters, write up reports on the election, interview candidates, make

predictions, and take popularity polls. Finally, all the children vote for a president for the fantasy island, or for the group of islands if the class has more than one.

LANGUAGE

Future: *will, going to*; past simple and past perfect; reported speech; present perfect; vocabulary of newspaper headlines; *opinion poll, manifesto,* and so on.

SKILLS

Making a speech; asking questions.

MATERIALS

Coloured paper (you will need as many colours as there are political parties); pens; glue; scissors; tape; staplers and staples. Samples of headlines for the reporters, such as 'Scandal! Candidate linked with crime ring', and so on; a strong cardboard box; photocopies of timetables A and B.

PREPARATION

1 Photocopy timetables A and B.
2 Arrange the classroom so that there is a large space in the centre of the room with areas for the candidates and reporters to base themselves.
3 Prepare a ballot paper with the names of the candidates and their political parties.
4 Make a ballot box (a closed cardboard box with a hole in the top for children to post their votes in).
5 Collect photographs or a television video of a recent local election to introduce the topic.

IN CLASS

1 Explain to the children that they are going to elect a president for their island(s).
2 Using examples from their own country or countries, make sure the children understand the following vocabulary: *party, slogan, manifesto, opinion poll, rosette, banner, press conference, scandal, ballot box, to vote, a vote, politician, candidate.* You can encourage the children to use their dictionaries to find translations in their language.
3 Divide the children into 'reporters' and 'political parties'. Each political party should consist of four members: the candidate, candidate's husband or wife, and two other members of the party. The children make labels to identify themselves. There should be one reporter to each political party.
4 Put the reporters into pairs and tell them to choose the name of their newspaper.
5 Explain that the children have to follow a tight time schedule, with deadlines. Give out sheets with timings (see sheets A and B). Go through the time schedule with the children to make sure that they understand what they have to do. Explain that they will be voting for a president at the end of the lesson.

Sheet A

Timetable—political parties

Minutes	Instructions
0–10	Get into groups of four. Decide the name of your political party. Choose your candidate, candidate's spouse, and two party members. Make an identity badge for each of you. For your party choose: – a colour – a symbol – a slogan. Make a poster and stick it on the wall. It must show: – the name of your party – the name of your candidate – your slogan, symbol, and colour.
10–30	Write out your manifesto together on a large sheet of paper. Make at least five promises. Stick your manifesto on the wall. Be prepared to answer questions from the reporters while you are doing this.
30–40	Have a look at the manifestos written by the other parties. Make some rosettes and/or banners for the party to use at the press conference. Check the opinion polls.
40–60	Read the reports written by the reporters. Prepare some questions to ask the other candidates at the press conference. Make sure each member of your party has one question to ask.
60–70	**The press conference** All the candidates sit at the front of the room with the reporters. Reporters ask each candidate a series of questions. Other members of the party form the audience.
70–80	The audience asks the candidates some questions.
80–90	Read the final opinion poll! Everyone votes! The election result is announced.

Sheet B

Timetable—reporters

Minutes	Instructions
0–20	Get into pairs.
	Decide the name of your newspaper.
	Make an identity badge.
	Check to see what the slogans, colours, and symbols are for each of the political parties.
	Find out the names of the candidates.
	Write a short report on the things you've found out and put it on the wall.
	Display an opinion poll on the wall.
20–30	Look at the manifestos written by the political parties.
	Quickly interview each candidate and other members of the party. See if you can find out some scandal.
30–50	Write a report about the political parties, try to include some scandal.
	Put up an opinion poll to show who you think might be in the lead.
50–60	Work with **all** the reporters.
	Choose one person to organize the press conference. This person must act as the conference co-ordinator.
	Prepare some questions to ask the candidates at the press conference.
	Decide on the questions each of you will ask. You should ask at least one question each.
	Put one reporter in charge of writing the final opinion poll.
60–70	**The press conference**
	All the candidates sit at the front of the room with the reporters.
	Reporters ask each candidate a series of questions.
	Other members of the party form the audience.
70–80	The audience asks the candidates some questions.
	One reporter writes the final opinion poll.
80–90	Read the final opinion poll!
	Everyone votes!
	The election result is announced.

6 Start the children off. Move around the groups and make sure everyone is working closely to their deadlines. Do not allow them extra time; make them work under pressure. Allow the children to work together on their own, but ensure that the timescale is followed. Shout out warnings at regular intervals, for example: *Five minutes to interviews with reporter. Look at the latest opinion polls on the walls.*

7 Hold the election and announce the results very formally, announcing the loser first.

5.10   Fantasy island poetry book

LEVEL	**Intermediate and above**
AGE GROUP	12–14
TIME	**60–90 minutes**
DESCRIPTION	The children complete a number of simple creative writing tasks, leading to the production of a variety of poems in different styles on the 'Fantasy island' theme. One of these poems could be selected as the national anthem of the island, and be set to music, if appropriate. A 'Fantasy Island Poetry Book' can be produced, containing examples of all the children's work.
LANGUAGE	Second conditional: *If I were … I would/could …* ; recycled language from the other activities.
SKILLS	Creative writing.
MATERIALS	Writing paper and pens or pencils; felt pens or crayons; large sheets of paper.
PREPARATION	Write some examples of the kinds of poems you are going to ask the children to produce.
IN CLASS	**Activity 1 Acrostic**

1 Explain to the class that they are going to write some simple poems on the theme of their fantasy island.
2 Begin with an 'acrostic' based on the name of the island or some other relevant word, for example, the name of a national hero from activity 5.5 'Celebrity guests'.

> *Dunwood island*
>
> **D**ark mystical creatures swim
> **U**nder the sea at
> **N**ight
> **W**hile
> **O**ver the
> **O**ceans float the
> **D**reams of the islanders.

3 Ask the children to create their own acrostics. They can choose to do so individually, or in pairs, or groups. The poems can be very simple.

> *Sea*
>
> **S**and
> **E**verywhere
> **A**lways

4 Set a time limit of 5–10 minutes, then ask the children to read their poems aloud for the rest of the class.

Activity 2 Diamonds

1 Show the children an example of a diamond poem.

River

Deep   Dark

Fast   Flowing   Frothing

Dangerous   Exciting   Mysterious   Freezing

Icy   Snowy   High

Soaring   Bright

Mountain

2 Choose two contrasting words, for example: *mountain/river, love/hate, war/peace, ice/fire*. These words make the first and last lines; between them adjectives form a pattern linking the two words.

3 Encourage the children to work in groups to produce diamond poems. It generally helps to brainstorm ideas and pool vocabulary. Each group should select two contrasting words and use the model supplied to produce their own poem. These can be written in poster form, on a large piece of paper using coloured pens to emphasize the contrast between the words (see highlighted words above). You can display the poems on the walls.

Activity 3 Draw a Poem

1 Ask the children to imagine one object they would take with them if they were shipwrecked on a desert island. Make a list on the board. Possible objects you could suggest might be torches, radios, sun-hats, and umbrellas.

2 Show this example on the board. Practise the structure: *If I were shipwrecked I would take … . I could …* . The whole class choose one of the items, and describe it in writing, trying to set the words out to form the shape of the object, as in this 'T-shirt' poem:

If I were ship wre   cked on an island I
would take my f   avourite T-shirt w
hich I bought at th   e Hard Rock Café
in London because   it's white and made
                of cotton which is excel
                lent for hot weather a
                nd I could even go swim
                ming in it and it would
                protect me from the sun.
                If I saw a ship or a plane
                in the distance I could ta
                ke it off and make a flag
                with it to wave and cry
                for help. SOS SOS SOS!!!!

3 In pairs, the children choose their own item and 'draw' their own poem. Display them.

Instead of writing about their object, the children can write the single word in a way that illustrates the characteristics of the object.

```
      m  b  r
   u     l     e
         l
         a
```

Activity 4 Fantasy love songs

This is the activity which is most likely to lead to the creation of an island 'National Anthem'. The idea is to produce a list of sentences which describe what it feels like to be without something or somebody.

1 Give the children an example:

Without my island

Me *without my island* *is like the sea without the shore*
Like …

2 Elicit more ideas from the children (for example, the sky without stars, like a postcard without a stamp, like fish without chips).

3 When the children have all understood the basic principle, ask them, individually or in groups, to create their own 'Without my island' poem. Specify the length, for example, a minimum of six lines and a maximum of ten. Ask them to write their poems out on a big sheet of paper for display.

4 When all the groups have finished, invite the children to read their work aloud. Ask the class to vote for their favourite poem, which can then be selected as the 'Fantasy Island National Anthem'.

Me without my island is like the sea without the shore
Like the night sky without stars
Like a plate without food
Like Prince Charming without Cinderella
Like a ship without a sail
Like a child without a home.

The chosen poem could be set to music—using either a familiar melody, or one the children have created. The entire collection of poems can be presented in book form, or recorded on to cassette and shown or played to other classes.

5.11 Island news

LEVEL	**Intermediate and above**
AGE GROUP	**12–14**
TIME	**60 minutes upwards**
DESCRIPTION	The children produce a 'Fantasy island newspaper' using items based on the results of the previous project activities.
LANGUAGE	Revision of all structures covered in previous activities.
SKILLS	Organization and groupwork.
MATERIALS	Large sheets of white paper (at least A3 size); paints, crayons, or felt pens.
PREPARATION	Take in some examples of magazines and newspapers, to help the children decide what format they are going to follow. It is best to do this activity after the children have already completed some or all of the previous fantasy island activities.

IN CLASS

1 Tell the children they are going to produce their own newspaper, and give them some real papers and magazines to look at. Explain that they do not actually need to *read* any of these examples, but you would like them to decide which kind of layout and style they would like to copy.

2 Ask the children to give you examples of the kind of items they can find in the newspapers they are looking through, for example: news reports, interviews, horoscopes, advertisements.

3 Ask them to think about whether any of the project activities they have already completed could be included in the class newspaper. They should come up with the following but if they do not, you could help them by making suggestions:

   5.2 The island flag could go on the front of the newspaper as part of the front page logo.

   5.3 A report could be produced on the 'sighting' of one of these strange island inhabitants, together with interviews with witnesses and 'photographs'/illustrations.

   5.4 There could be a page of advertisements selling the houses created previously, together with descriptions and illustrations.

   5.5 The children could interview each other about the visitors, or write an imaginary interview with the celebrity.

5.6 The children could write an article reporting on the celebrity's visit.

5.7 A financial report on the state of the island currency, together with a table of exchange rates. If the children are feeling more creative, they could invent a financial scandal or any other kind of scandal involving the island's national heroes.

5.8 A travel feature could include reports on dream holidays.

5.9 The election results and a profile of the new president, together with an interview and photograph could be printed. A report on the president's manifesto could be written, using future time to describe the promises made to the electorate.

5.10 The newspaper could run a competition, and publish the winning entries.

4 Divide the class into pairs or groups. Allocate, or allow each group to choose, a task from the above (or do something different if they have a good idea for something that could be included in the newspaper, for example, a fantasy island recipe, or horoscopes). You can elect an editor, or editorial team, responsible for deciding on layout and what goes where in the finished newspaper. You may decide to do this yourself if time is limited.

5 Tell the children how long they have to discuss and produce their contribution. Items can be word processed or handwritten but, if pages are to be photocopied, black ink on white paper is the best combination.

6 Get the editorial team to collect in the finished articles and compile them into a newspaper. You can glue them on to sheets of A4/A3 paper and photocopy them for each class member. If you do not have access to a photocopier, the individual pages of the newspaper can be displayed on the classroom walls until everybody has had a chance to read them. They can then be stapled together to make the newspaper, which can be kept somewhere safe by the teacher, and perhaps 'raffled' to a member of the class at the end of the course.

VARIATION

If time permits, or you wish to devote more time to this activity, each group can produce its own newspaper and, instead of contributing one item only, can work on a range of items from the suggested list above, adding their own supplementary ideas as appropriate. There could be a 'prize' for the best newspaper or magazine.

_____

_____

_____

_____

_____

_____

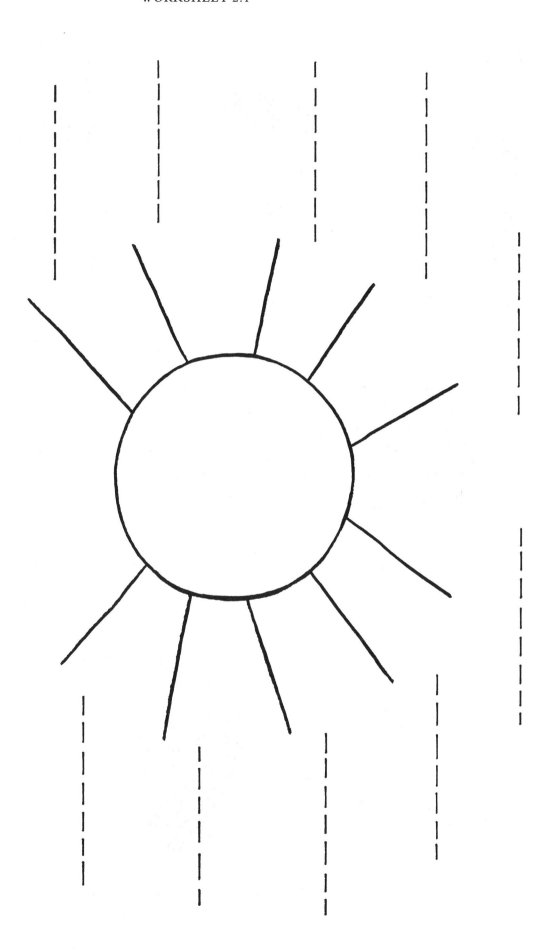

_____ went _____ the _____

_____ the _____

and _____ _____ the _____ .

Then he went _____ the _____
and _____ the _____ .

He played _____ the _____ .

He swam _____ the _____ ,
chased the _____

and he ate some _____ .

He went _____ the _____ and

Then he fell _____ the _____

_____ the _____ .

and he couldn't get out.

Locations:

The scientist's laboratory — photograph in
the corner of the classroom by the window.

Need: some test tubes and bits of cardboard cut
and painted to look like pieces of a rocket being built.

In space — paint a picture of the rocket
travelling through space, with lots of stars and
Mars in the distance. Take a photograph of the
painting.

Need: paint, large piece of paper, silver stars to
stick on, a book to copy picture of Mars.

On Mars — photograph in the dry
sandy area of the playground.

Need: a few plants and rocks for the
scientists to hold.

In the aliens' living room — photograph a
corner of the classroom.

Need: tablecloth, plates, cups, cakes.

The scientist's office — photograph of the
school office and computer.

Need: telephone, computer.

Characters:

A scientist – a photograph of Julia, wearing a wig, a white beard, and glasses.

Need: a white wig, cotton wool to make a beard, a white scientist's coat.

Two aliens – a painting, green skin, three eyes, a big mouth, four arms, two short legs, lots of toes.

Need: paints, very large piece of paper.

The aliens' family – a painting, two parents and three children.

Need: paints, very large piece of paper.

Story Board

The scientist is building his rocket in his laboratory. (Photograph in classroom)

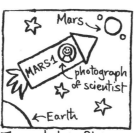

The rocket is flying through space towards Mars. (Photograph of painting of rocket - stick on Mars and Earth.)

The rocket is landing on Mars. (Photograph in playground - stick on picture of rocket)

The scientist is collecting rocks and plants. (Photograph in playground - stick on thought bubble.)

The aliens are hiding and watching the scientist. (Photograph of painting of aliens - stick on thought bubble.)

The scientist is looking shocked because the aliens are coming towards him. (Photograph in playground.)

The aliens are saying 'Hello'. (Photograph of painting of aliens - stick on words bubbles.)

The scientist is saying 'Hello'. (Photograph in playground - stick on words bubble.)

The aliens and the scientist are having tea together. (Photograph at table in classroom - stick on words bubble.)

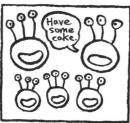

The aliens and the scientist are having tea together. (Photograph of alien family - stick on words bubble.)

The aliens are waving goodbye. (Photograph in playground - picture of rocket stuck on.)

The rocket is flying back to earth. (Photograph of space painting - turn rocket other way round.)

The scientist is typing an e-mail to the aliens. (Photograph of school office - stick words on computer screen "Dear friends...")

The aliens are building a space rocket. (Photograph of painting of aliens - stick on picture of rocket and words bubble.)

The End! (Photograph of our group holding "The End" - stick on our names.)

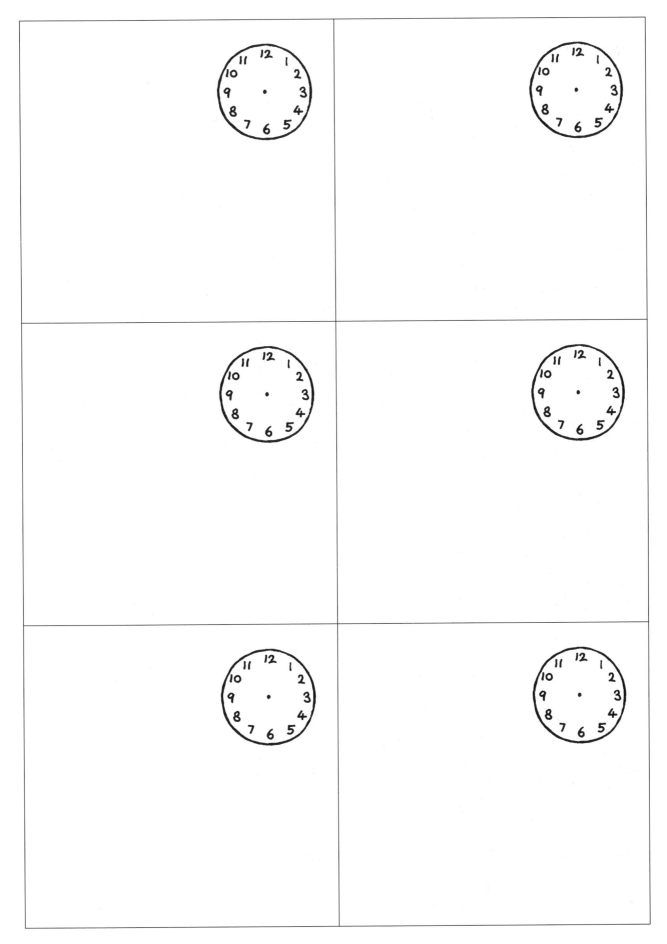

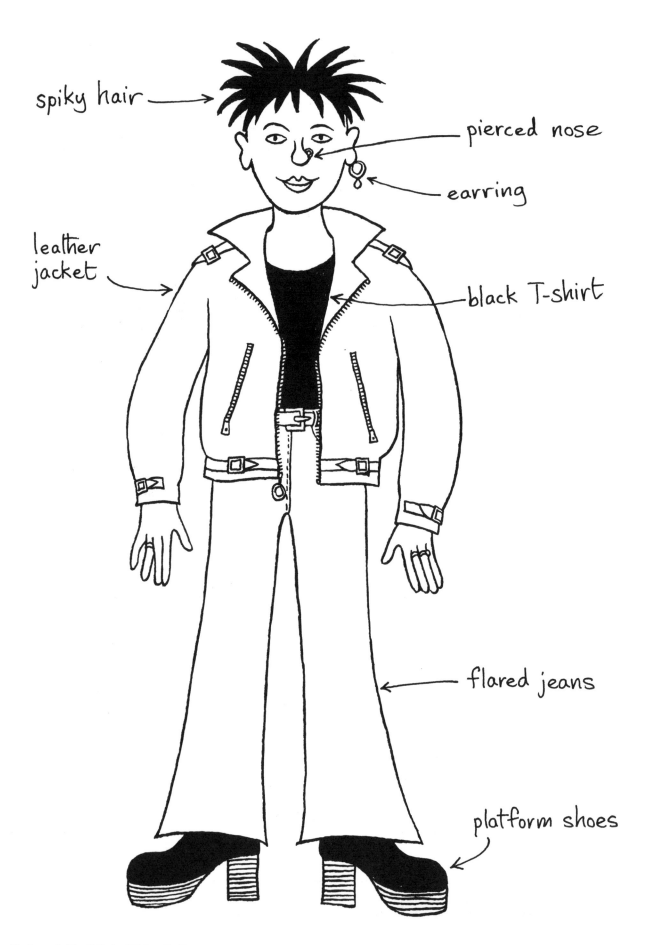

spiky hair

pierced nose

earring

leather jacket

black T-shirt

flared jeans

platform shoes

♪♩♬ Mystery Band ♪♩♫♪

	Name	Which instrument does he/she play?	What is the last letter of the name?
A			
B			
C			
D			
E			
F			
G			
H			

Name of the band: _ _ _ _ / _ _ _ _

dolphin   elephant   mouse   hedgehog   horse

leopard   snake   lizard   frog   newt   owl

sparrow   eagle   spider   ant   butterfly

mammal   reptile   amphibian   bird   insect

Further reading

Below is a brief list of books that teachers may find useful. Although very few of them are specifically about using projects with young learners, many of the ideas and activities in these books can be adapted for use within a project framework.

Methodology

Argondizzo, C. 1992. *Children in Action*. London: Prentice Hall. A thorough rationale, and a rich collection of practical activities indexed by school subject.

Brewster, J., G. Ellis, and **D. Girard.** 1992. *The Primary English Teacher's Guide*. Harmondsworth: Penguin. Examines the development of language teaching to young children. It contains teaching techniques and learning strategies, practical suggestions, and lists resources available.

Dunn, O. 1983. *Beginning English with Young Children*. London: Macmillan.

Dunn, O. 1984. *Developing English with Young Children*. London: Macmillan. These two books provide answers to common problems experienced by teachers of English who work with young learners.

Halliwell, S. 1992. *Teaching English in the Primary Classroom*. Harlow: Longman. Discusses the special abilities of young children and includes activities to practise language.

Halliwell, S. and **L. Kissinger.** *Primary English Language Teaching Video*. Harlow: Longman/The Bell Educational Trust. A teacher training video which provides support for teachers with large classes of young learners.

Hutchinson, T. 1991. *Introduction to Project Work*. Oxford: Oxford University Press. Techniques which can be adapted for young learners.

Moon, J. 1999. *Children Learning English*. Oxford: Macmillan Heinemann. An introduction to the theoretical concepts that underpin good classroom practice.

Phillips, S. 1993. *Young Learners*. Oxford: Oxford University Press. Advice and ideas for teaching children aged 3 to 6. Over 80 activities including games, songs, drama, stories , and arts and crafts.

Vale, D. and **A. Feunteun.** 1995. *Teaching Children English*. Cambridge: Cambridge University Press. A training course for teachers of English to children.

Wood, D. 1988. *How Children Think and Learn: The Social Contexts of Cognitive Development*. Oxford: Blackwell. A useful insight into how children learn.

Topics

Any Usborne book, for example:

Tyler, J. 1981. *Usborne Book of World Geography.* London: Usborne. These books are designed for native speakers, but can be used with second language learners.

Crafts

Bawden, J. 1991. *101 Things to make.* Hemel Hempstead: Simon and Schuster Young Books. Craft ideas with lots of pictures.

Bryant, D. 1990. *Things to make: 5 -year-olds.* London: Piccolo. Games, monsters, recipes, word games, and masks.

Hale, K. 1985. *Some Crafty Things to Do.* Oxford: Oxford Education. Crafts from around the world: batik, musical instruments, and cooking.

Grammar and vocabulary

Lewis, G. and **G. Bedson.** 1999. *Games for Children.* Oxford: Oxford University Press. A collection of games for children 4–11, including card games, board games, and co-operative and competitive games.

Rinvolucri, M. 1985. *Grammar Games* . Cambridge: Cambridge University Press.

Rinvolucri, M. and **P. Davis.** 1995. *More Grammar Games.* Cambridge: Cambridge University Press. Both these books contain ideas to make grammar more exciting. Designed for older children, but many of the games are adaptable.

Ur, P. 1988. *Grammar Practice Activities.* Cambridge: Cambridge University Press. This book has a practical introduction and ideas for practising and presenting structures.

Games, drama, and activities

Palim, J. and **P. Power.** 1990. *Jamboree: Communication Activities for Children.* Harlow: Longman. A book of activities with photocopiable worksheets.

Phillips, S. 1999. *Drama with Children.* Oxford: Oxford University Press. 'Resource Books for Teachers' series. Lots of fun and interesting ideas for using drama in the classroom.

Retter, C. and **N. Valls.** 1984. *Bonanza.* Harlow: Longman. Language games for children with colour picture cards.

Toth, M. 1995. *Children's Games.* Oxford: Heinemann. Games with photocopiable worksheets.

Using Stories

Ellis, G. and **J. Brewster** (ed). 1991. *The Storytelling Handbook for Primary Teachers.* Harmondsworth: Penguin English. Ideas for using authentic story-books with young learners.

Morgan, J. and **M. Rinvolucri.** 1983. *Once Upon a Time: using stories in the language classroom.* Cambridge: Cambridge University Press. These activity ideas can be adapted for use in the primary classroom.

Wright, A. 1995. *Storytelling with Children.* Oxford: Oxford University Press. 'Resource Books for Teachers' series. Original ideas for using stories with children learning English.

Wright, A. 1995. *Creating Stories with Children.* Oxford: Oxford University Press. Ideas for encouraging creativity, confidence, fluency, and accuracy with children aged 7–14.

Story-books

Ahlberg, J. and **A. Ahlberg.** 1982. *Funnybones.* London: HarperCollins. A rhyming book which includes characters from traditional stories.

Biro, V. 1985. *The Three Little Pigs.* Oxford: Oxford University Press. Traditional stories for native speakers. This book contains colourful illustrations.

Bradman, T. and **M. Chamberlain.** 1989. *Look Out! He's Behind You! The story of Little Red Riding Hood.* London: Mammoth. A lift-the-flap version of the children's story.

Campbell, R. 1982. *Dear Zoo.* Harmondsworth: Penguin. A lift-the-flap book about choosing a pet.

Carle, E. 1970. *The Very Hungry Caterpillar.* Harmondsworth: Penguin. This famous story is available in several languges and on video.

Hill, E. 1983. *Where's Spot?* Harmondsworth: Penguin. Story of a little dog on his birthday.

Hutchins, P. 1974. *Rosie's Walk* Harmondsworth: Penguin. A funny story about Rosie the hen, who goes for a walk but doesn't know a fox is following her.

Nicholl, H. and **J. Pienkowski.** 1972. *Meg and Mog .* London: Penguin. The adventures of the witch and her cat.

Nicholl, H. and **J. Pienkowski.** 1985. *Meg's Eggs.* London: Penguin A well-known story about a witch and some dinosaurs. A popular topic with young children.

Sendak, M. 1964. *Where the Wild Things Are.* London: HarperCollins. A scary story about weird creatures. Very popular with native speaker children of all ages.

Songs and Rhymes

Byrne, J. and **A. Waugh.** 1982. *Jingle Bells* Oxford: Oxford University Press. A book and cassette of traditional songs for young learners of English.

Graham, C. 1979. *Jazz Chants for Children.* New York: Oxford University Press. Jazz chants help learners with stress, rhythm, pronunciation, and structures.

Graham, C. 1988. *Jazz Chant Fairytales*. New York: Oxford University Press. These are traditional stories told in verse. Perhaps most suitable for children with several years of English.

Hadley, H. 1992. *Inspirations for Poetry*. Leamington Spa: Scholastic Publications. Ideas for helping children to write their own poems.

English Nursery Rhymes for Young Learners. 1986. Harlow: Longman. The best known nursery rhymes, with music and suggestions for the teacher.

Murphey, T. 1992. *Music and Songs*. Oxford: Oxford University Press. 'Resource Books for Teachers' series. This contains a chapter on young learners, and other activities are adaptable.

Super Songs. 1997. Oxford: Oxford University Press. Cassette and book of 27 traditional songs for young learners of English.

Traverso, P. 1992. ' Writing Rhymes with children' *Jet* Vol. 2 No. 3, Issue 6. Using songs to teach English.

Dictionaries

Hill, L. and **C. Innes.** 1981. *Oxford Children's Picture Dictionary*. Oxford: Oxford University Press.

Maidment, S. 1996. *Oxford Picture Power Dictionary*. Oxford: Oxford University Press.

Vale, D. and **S. Mullaney.** 1996. *The Cambridge Picture Dictionary*. Cambridge: Cambridge University Press.

Wright, A. 1985. *Collins Picture Dictionary for Young Learners*. London and Glasgow: Collins ELT.

All these dictionaries have clear pictures to explain vocabulary on the topics in the projects.

Pictures and Flashcards

Thomas, S. and **P. Sanday.** *Mini flashcards Resource Pack*. Harlow: Longman. Eight sets of cards and a photocopiable resource book of games and activities.

Wright, A. 1993. *1000 Pictures for Teachers to copy*. Harlow: Longman. Very simple pictures that teachers can copy. The book is organized by theme, and grammatically.

Indexes

Language

Adjectives 2.5, 2.6, 3.7, 4.4, 4.6
Adverbs 3.5, 3.6, 3.10, 4.3, 4.6
Articles 1.3, 1.5
Be 1.1, 1.3, 1.4, 1.5, 1.6, 1.8, 2.2
Can (requests) 1.3, 1.11
Comparatives 4.7, 4.10, 5.8
Conditionals 5.10
Going to 4.7, 5.9, 5.11
Have got 2.3, 2.5, 5.3
Imperatives 1.2, 1.7, 5.8
Instructions 3.9, 3.10
Introductions 2.4, 2.8
Invitations 1.10, 5.5
Likes and dislikes 1.9, 2.6, 2.9, 4.1
Linking words 3.4, 3.5
Making suggestions 1.9
Modals 1.2, 1.3, 1.11, 3.3, 5.8, 5.9, 5.11
Offering 1.11
Passive 5.4
Past continuous 3.2, 3.4, 3.5, 3.6, 3.7, 3.8, 3.10, 4.1, 5.11
Past perfect 5.7, 5.9, 5.11
Past simple 1.5, 2.7, 3.1, 3.2, 3.3, 3.4, 3.5, 3.6, 3.10, 4.1, 4.2, 4.7, 5.7, 5.9, 5.11
Possessive 's' 1.6, 4.10
Possessive adjectives 1.7, 2.3, 2.5, 2.6
Prepositions 1.6, 2.2, 2.7, 4.9
Present continuous 2.5, 3.2, 3.8, 3.10, 3.10, 4.4, 4.5, 4.9, 5.8, 5.11
Present perfect 5.9, 5.11
Present simple 2.5, 3.2, 3.8, 3.10, 4.1, 4.2, 4.3, 4.9, 5.1, 5.3, 5.4, 5.6, 5.8, 5.11
Questions 1.1, 1.4, 1.6, 1.8, 1.10, 1.11, 2.1, 2.2, 2.3, 2.5, 2.6, 2.7, 2.8
Reported speech 5.9, 5.11
Requests 1.11, 3.9, 3.10
Short answers 1.8
Superlatives 4.10, 5.8
Time 1.10, 5.6
There is, there are 2.1
This 1.3 1.5
Will 3.3, 5.9, 5.11

Topics

Animals 1.2, 1.3, 1.4, 1.5, 1.6, 1.7, 1.12, 2.6, 3.2, 3.3, 3.5, 5.3
Birthdays 1.1, 1.12
Body 1.3, 1.6, 1.7, 1.12, 2.4, 2.6, 5.3
Buildings 5.4
Cartoons 2.1, 3.1, 4.3
Cassettes/CDs 4.1
Clothes 2.4, 2.5, 4.2, 4.4, 4.5, 4.9
Colours 1.4, 1.7, 2.1, 2.2, 2.3, 2.4, 2.5, 4.4, 5.2
Cooking 1.11
Countries 4.7
Days of the week 1.10
Descriptions 2.4, 2.5, 3.1, 3.2, 3.7, 4.1, 4.2, 4.4, 4.5, 5.5
Drink 1.9, 1.11, 1.12
Elections 5.9
Family 2.3, 3.2
Fashion 4.4, 4.5
Films 3.9
Flags 5.2
Food 1.4, 1.9, 1.11, 1.12
Furniture 2.1, 2.2
Games 1.2, 1.4, 1.6, 1.12, 2.2, 2.8
Geographical features 4.7, 5.1, 5.2, 5.4, 5.6, 5.8
Hobbies 2.8
Holidays 3.2, 5.8
Homes 2.1–2.10, 5.3, 5.4
Insects 3.3
Inviting 1.10, 5.5
Islands 5.1–5.11
Jobs 3.9, 5.7
Magazines 4.11, 5.11
Maps 5.1
Masks 1.3, 1.12
Money 5.7
Music 4.1–4.11
Musical instruments 4.6, 4.9
Nationalities 5.2
Newspapers 5.9, 5.11
Numbers 1.1, 1.12, 2.1, 2.5, 4.7, 5.7
Parks 2.7
Parties 1.1–1.12
People 2.4, 2.5, 3.7, 4.2, 4.9, 5.5
Photo-stories 3.1–3.10
Pirates 1.2, 1.12
Poetry 5.10
Points of the compass 5.1
Pop bands 4.1–4.11
Rooms 2.1, 2.2, 5.4
Sea 1.2, 1.12
Shapes 5.2
Ships 1.2, 1.12
Songs 1.5, 1.12, 3.3, 4.8
Sports 2.8
Stories 3.1–3.10
Story genres 3.5
Tourism 5.6, 5.8
Weather 4.7, 5.4

OXFORD
UNIVERSITY PRESS

Dear Teacher

We would like your views on how best to develop the *Resource Books for Teachers* series. We would be very grateful if you could fill in this questionnaire and return it to the address at the bottom. We are offering a free OUP wallchart to everyone who returns this form, and a free Resource Book each for the ten most informative replies received every month.

About yourself

Your name _____

Address _____

_____

_____

Are you: ☐ A teacher?　　☐ A teacher trainer?　　☐ A trainee teacher?

Other? (Please specify) _____

What type of establishment do you work in? _____

What age are your students?　　☐ 3–6　　☐ 6–12　　☐ 12–17　　☐ 18+

How many students per class?　　☐ under 15　　☐ 15–30　　☐ over 30

Which teachers' resource book(s) do you use most (from any publisher)?

_____

Which topic(s) would you most like to have covered in a Resource Book for Teachers?

_____

_____

About *Projects with Young Learners*

Do you read the Introduction? Yes/No

Do you find it useful? Why? _____

_____

Which activities do you find most useful? Why?

_____

_____

Is there anything you **don't** like about the book? _____

_____

We have changed the size of this book and hope you like it and the new cover design.

Which size do you prefer?　☐ This size　　☐ Don't mind

　　　　　　　　　　☐ Other? (Please specify) _____

Do you photocopy the worksheets?　　Yes/No

Any other comments? (*You can continue your comments on a separate sheet if you wish.*)

_____

_____

_____

_____

Please send your reply to:
Julia Sallabank
Senior Editor, ELT
Oxford University Press
Great Clarendon Street
Oxford
OX2 6DP
UK

Thank you very much for taking the time to answer this questionnaire.

Which wallchart would you prefer?

☐ Map of the UK and world　　　　☐ The zany zoo (primary)

☐ Map of the USA　　　　　　　　☐ Town scene with worksheets (primary)

☐ English sounds (IPA symbols)

Which Resource Book for Teachers would you prefer? (See the list on pages ?.)